Also available at all good book stores

9781785317927

9781801500630

9781801500067

9781801500500

9781785318245

9781801500586

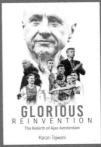

9781801500692

9781801501323

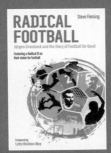

9781801501149

IN THE
SHADOW OF
BENBULBEN

IN THE
SHADOW OF
BENBULBEN

Dixie Dean
at Sligo Rovers

Paul Little

First published by Pitch Publishing, 2022

Pitch Publishing
9 Donnington Park,
85 Birdham Road,
Chichester,
West Sussex,
PO20 7AJ
www.pitchpublishing.co.uk
info@pitchpublishing.co.uk

ISBN 978 1 80150 102 6

Typesetting and origination by Pitch Publishing
Printed and bound in India by Replika Press Pvt. Ltd.

Contents

For Mam, Dad and all my family –
Hope this makes you smile.

To my lovely wife, Trish, who I accept
will probably never get past this page,
and our wonderful children – Emily,
Kate, Noah and Joe –
Keep being who you are and never
stop dreaming.

'Dixie was the greatest centre-forward there ever will be. His record of goalscoring is the most amazing thing under the sun. He belongs in the company of the supremely great, like Beethoven, Shakespeare and Rembrandt.'

Bill Shankly – Liverpool FC

Foreword

DIXIE DEAN is revered throughout the footballing world and beyond as a goalscoring legend.

Dean's ability to make the most difficult task of all on a football pitch, scoring goals, look easy surpassed all who had gone before and all who were still to come.

Despite achieving footballing records that to this day remain unbeaten, he remained humble – an advocate for doing the right thing and speaking up for others whose voices may not be heard. He was loved as much for his personality and film star looks as he was for his skill.

He was a highly prized player, but towards the end of his career he chose to go to Sligo on the west coast of Ireland.

The people of Sligo were thrilled at the prospect of this star coming to play for them and he was treated like a king. Dixie repaid that kindness through his crowd-pulling appearances and, of course, his goals.

Dixie spent less than six months in Sligo, but the place always held a special place in his heart – and I have been proud to carry on what my grandad started and continue to support the Bit O' Red whenever and however I can.

Melanie Prentice,
granddaughter of
William Ralph 'Dixie' Dean

1

Dixie and Sligo – A Fairy Tale Almost Lost in Time

THE LEAGUE of Ireland turned 100 years old in 2021. One hundred years that have seen clubs, players, managers and football grounds come and go. For all that the beautiful game in Ireland has been ignored and neglected, even by the 'football public' for almost half of its existence now, the League and so many of its early members have prevailed. Indeed, in recent seasons, there have been signs of a revival in interest. 'Sold out' signs at Dalymount Park, big crowds at Tallaght Stadium and elsewhere.

Unfortunately, that recovery came to a dramatic halt in March 2020 as the world was hit by the COVID-19 pandemic – an outbreak that has shaped each and every one of our lives since.

The battle against the virus continues. Ireland was in the midst of a devastating 'third wave' when I began to write this book. When I'd finally dotted the i's and crossed the t's, the Delta variant was threatening a fourth. Football here returned in August 2020 for a truncated season – but without the fans, the lifeblood of Irish clubs. Government money, the admirable efforts of supporters and owners, streaming revenue and some serious cost-cutting kept the show on the road. Finally, in the summer of 2021, the first fans were allowed to trickle back through our turnstiles. Hopes for a return to normality on the terraces and in our lives rest on the efficaciousness of vaccines.

Such a contrast to the last weekends before the pandemic struck – characterised by a buoyant feel to the beginning of the 2020 term. The sense that something was stirring was perhaps best illustrated by a pulsating encounter between champions Dundalk and their Dublin rivals Shamrock Rovers that sold out the latter's south-side venue (the first league sell-out at the Tallaght Stadium), wowed an enthralled television audience and saw a Jordan Flores strike for the Lilywhites (Dundalk Football Club, for readers outside of the Emerald Isle) go viral, drawing admiring glances and nods from across the world.

From a football perspective, the gradual return to the 'old normal' suggests that the renewed interest in Irish football was merely put on ice by the pandemic. Demand for tickets, albeit at reduced-capacity fixtures, has been strong. Naturally, there is pent-up demand for even the simplest of life's pleasures. But there is also a feeling that something has changed in how the game on this island is being perceived. Perhaps it's down to a long-overdue realisation that it's possible to be in the thrall of the English Premier League while at the same time finding time for local fare.

For some, myself included, there has been a falling out of love with 'big club, big time' football across the water and elsewhere. The tiresome, overbearing bombast and the growing sense of alienation from a game increasingly dominated by often unsavoury, mega-rich owners have played their part. Ties have not been severed. It's never that simple. But Irish domestic football offers a welcome kitchen-sink antidote to the glamorous but tawdry soap from across the water and across the continent.

Undoubtedly, few will look back on the pandemic years with any great fondness. That said, many people will reflect on how the curtailing of so many of the daily activities we took for granted and that often cluttered our lives served to create unexpected, and not unwelcome, time for other pursuits. Projects once put on very long and often lengthening fingers came unexpectedly to see the light of day. This book is one such 'child' of the pandemic.

The inspiration has been twofold. First, the very thought of one of the game's most legendary exponents living and playing in the far west of Ireland is both beguiling and romantic.

In late January 1939, William Ralph 'Dixie' Dean, the greatest goalscorer English football had and has ever known, a genuine superstar of the game, came out of what had been a very short retirement to go and play for little Sligo Rovers – possibly the most westerly outpost of European football at the time.

Had Dean gone to a Dublin side, then maybe the move might have had more logic to it. Crossing the water to the Irish capital, just across the Irish Sea from Dean's Birkenhead home, would have made at least some sense. The trade between the two ports and the many Irish who had settled along the Mersey had bound Dublin and Liverpool together after all. And, of course, the city possessed the country's biggest and best-resourced clubs.

But the switch to a small market town on Ireland's wild Atlantic seaboard – a town with a population less than half the size of an average Everton home gate (the club with which Dean had made his name) – just catches the imagination. Sligo Rovers, the Bit O' Red as they are affectionately known, had only been founded 11 years before Dean's arrival and had only joined the League of Ireland in 1934. The club was and continues to be a co-operative venture owned by the people of Sligo and the surrounding area. And it remains the heartbeat of the town to this day. Dean's move to the club and the love affair it engendered is a story that deserves a detailed retelling. This I've sought to do.

The other reason for writing this book has been about redressing a balance. It saddens me how few stories we hear or read from the beautiful game's history here in Ireland. How few books are published on the endeavours, both domestic and European, of our football clubs. Perhaps the interest isn't there. But in a sport- and football-mad country, that is sad in itself.

One hundred years is a long time to be in operation, but the focus of the Irish football public has, for the last five decades at least, been centred on football in England and Scotland. Unsurprisingly, the heroes of the Irish game in that time reflect that orientation. Domestic football folklore has largely been ignored or forgotten and is rarely celebrated.

Compare that to how much we hear of the greats of our 'national sports' of Gaelic football and hurling. 'Not men, but giants,' went the advertising slogan some years back. And there's no doubt that this is how many see the admittedly fine exponents of these games. But without wanting to denigrate these traditional sporting pastimes, it is fair to say that those who display their fine arts at the elite levels of Gaelic games have never had their 'greatness' eroded or undermined by unflattering or often unfair comparison with counterparts in other countries, for there are none. But for the Association footballers here, failure to have proven yourself across the Irish Sea often sees legacies, stories, talent and achievements talked down and dismissed.

So telling the tale, no, the fairy tale, of 'Dixie' Dean coming to play in Ireland is an effort to redress the balance a little. A star coming in the opposite direction in a period of the game here where the gap between football in Ireland and its bigger neighbour hadn't stretched to the yawning chasm we see today. Indeed, in the 1930s and 1940s, there was a brisk football trade between the two islands, and it wasn't always the kind of one-way traffic you might imagine.

But it's true, Dean was no longer at his very best when he arrived on these shores. The wear and tear of a 16-year-long professional career, starting at Tranmere Rovers and startling in a golden period for Everton Football Club, had certainly taken a toll. That said, he was still only 32 when he first lined out for Sligo Rovers. And he went on to prove over his four months with the club that he was by no means a spent force who had travelled over just to pick up some handy pre-retirement money.

Whatever his intentions on moving to Yeats Country, whatever drove that decision, a bond grew between the legendary striker and the Connacht club that lasted long, long after his departure in that last summer before the outbreak of World War II. Tellingly, Dean was to look back in his memoirs on his time in Sligo as some of his happiest in the game – and he was to return as the club's guest of honour on cup final day some 30 years later in 1970. Indeed, the links between Sligo and Dean's family were once again movingly illustrated when his daughter Barbara, granddaughter Melanie and great-grandchildren Daniel and Scarlett were guests of the club as the Bit O' Red made their debut as Irish champions in the Champions League at the Showgrounds in July of 2013.

Clearly, there was a financial incentive for Dean to travel way out west. Compared with conditions today, football in the 1930s was a very different animal for players. Even the game's superstars typically had very little in their bank accounts when the time came to hang up their boots. Indeed, it's really only in the last 30 years that a top player could retire without ever having to worry about money again.

Having ended his playing days in England after the glories of Goodison Park and Everton and a brief and unhappy period with lowly Notts County, Dean moved into scouting and talent-spotting to earn a crust, acutely aware that short- and medium-term finance could prove a problem even for a footballing god. There simply was no safety net. He had a family to feed and knew just how difficult the world outside the game could be. The failure of a sports shop he had opened in his final season with Everton in 1937 had certainly made that plain. So when Sligo came calling, it was hardly surprising that when he realised his name still held currency he would attempt to capitalise on it.

And then there was the simple pull of the game, the green sward (or probably more often the brown mud and straw) and the ball. Having spent several months out of the game, in which his body had time to recover itself somewhat, perhaps he came to realise that he still had something to offer and that, well, he still just wanted to play.

That it was Sligo Rovers that benefited is befitting of the great pantomime that is football. Anything can happen, as they say, and for Rovers it did. Timing, such an important part of the game and one of Dixie's great gifts, was to prove generous to the club in creating one of the great stories of the Irish game. A tale that has been told in somewhat abridged fashion, as I found in my efforts to research it – but rarely in any sense of totality or in a way that left me satisfied. And so, in lockdown, with a little more time on my hands than I'd ever expected,

I decided to see if I could do that story (and the game on this island) just a little more justice. To see if I could bring it all to life.

* * *

In researching and writing the book, I've leaned very much on the newspaper reporting of the great centre-forward's half season with Sligo. The games, the engagements, the goals and the crowds – all seen through the eyes and told in the words of those reporters lucky enough to have seen him first-hand during that period.

Chief among them was the curiously bylined 'Volt' of the local *Sligo Champion* who recounted each and every game in his Saturday match reports and 'Soccer Causerie' column. With Sligo Rovers being primarily a 'Sunday team' (League of Ireland clubs in those days chose between Saturdays or Sundays for their home fixtures – the decisions driven by player availability and the day most suitable to the majority of their support), Volt's pieces tended to be delivered a week after each match, as the *Champion* was a weekly Saturday paper. In a way, that has proven more educational, illustrative and colourful, as the reporter had plenty of time to digest what he had seen at the Showgrounds, home of the Bit O' Red, or the other venues around the country graced by the legendary striker.

Similar pieces, often more immediate – a day after a fixture, for example – were available from the archives of the daily papers, the *Irish Independent*, the *Evening*

Herald, the *Cork Examiner*, the *Evening Echo* and the late lamented *Irish Press*. All delivered by likewise curiously named football writers ('WPM' of the *Independent*, the *Herald*'s 'NAT', 'Spectator' at the *Echo* and 'Socaro' of the *Irish Press*), and indeed presented in often familiar football parlance, showing how the game and how it is discussed by those who live for it or live off it hasn't actually changed that much in 80 years.

The pseudonyms on the football pages seem strange today in a time where football writers are often as famous as those they write about, transferring from paper to paper or website to website as the outlets battle for page views and circulation. But as writer and former sports journalist Paul Howard explained to me, back in Dean's day, it was typical for reporters to have such bylines and it was also common for those bylines to actually be more than one person!

'It was quite common in sports and social diary writing that a number of people would contribute to a particular column, and it would be published under a pseudonym, especially in horse racing. The names of individual journalists didn't really matter until about 100 years ago. If you look at papers outside of the last century, most of what was published was unbylined.' Quite a different picture today, where many football writers have supporters of their own!

Efforts to uncover who was behind these mysterious names proved largely fruitless. But perhaps that's as it should be, for if that's how they wanted it then, why should we look to unmask them now?

Whoever they were, much of this story is recounted through their words, scribbled and typed so long ago. And I owe its authenticity and much of its simple beauty to them.

Other sources include Nick Walsh's 1977 seminal biography of the player, *Dixie Dean – The Life Story of a Goalscoring Legend,* and *Dixie Uncut – The Lost Interview,* a volume based on a series of interviews with the player in the early 1970s serialised by the *Liverpool Echo* newspaper. Although between them, scarcely two pages on Dean's half season in Sligo are filled, both reference those days with a depth of feeling and genuine warmth. The value of both books for my purposes, however, lay in providing me with a greater insight into the man himself and the times in which he played.

Walsh's book is the only biography of Dixie Dean. That point alone is more than a little thought-provoking. Imagine a star of the game in more modern times producing or commissioning just the one book about his career! And imagine any player waiting the guts of 30 years after their finest moments before seeing such a tome appear on a shelf in a bookshop!

Walsh, like Dean, was a Birkenhead boy, born just eight years after his idol in 1915. This was his only-ever book – being for most of his career an executive officer in the Lord Chancellor's department in Liverpool and editor and producer of the *Court Officer,* the national journal representing the main staff association of the United Kingdom courts service. Walsh was a football enthusiast who reputedly spent a long time trying to persuade Dean as to the merits of such a book and to gain his cooperation in the endeavour.

The book itself is a little football gem, mined from the vaults of the Limerick library where it lay untouched since 11 September 1997 until I summoned it to my Wicklow home! In a way, that long period in which it was unread only added to my interest in Dean's story. The idea that one of such greatness, who held such fame, can gradually fade from people's consciousness and interest. And perhaps even more poignant was the note on the inner sleeve about the author himself that stated in very small and unprepossessing script, 'Shortly before publication of this book, the author, Nick Walsh, died suddenly at his home in Liverpool.'

How sad. A little tragedy. Knowing how tough it is to try and write while also holding down a day job and bringing up a family – and the achievement of attracting the interest of a publisher – poor Nick Walsh never got to see his book sitting proudly on a shelf in a shop. He may never even have held a copy in his hand.

In a way, my own scribbling is a monument to both men – a humble reminder of their very existence. (And maybe mine too!) Doubtless, however, this book will go the same way. Destined to gather dust, perhaps fittingly, in a Sligo library. Maybe one day it will be searched down by myself, or one of my progenies, in JR Hartley fashion! (Look him up on YouTube if you are too young to remember the Yellow Pages phone directory television ad.) If so, then so be it. Because at least in such a reality it will have been published and have had a little life of its own. And maybe it will have thrown a little colour into someone's life – even if it's most likely to only be my own or that of my ever-patient family and friends!

But a little colour is important. And it's important when reading this book. So as you read it, I ask that you try and see it in colour. See the bright red of the Sligo Rovers jersey, the greyish brown of the muck and mud of their Showgrounds pitch on a Sunday in late January, the ruddy faces of those in awe as a living legend takes to the field on a cold winter's day.

It's hard to do, I know. As a child, I found it hard to believe that in the classic movies of the 1940s and 1950s so beloved of my parents, people then lived and breathed in colour. The old *Pathé News* footage and the newspaper photographs of the time capture so much, yet render it somehow less real than our own experiences of the world because they are just shades of grey. But try and see it all in colour – the excited hubbub as Dixie Dean arrives at Sligo's train station, Dixie Dean emerging from the dressing rooms and running on to the football pitch at the Showgrounds, Dixie Dean playing golf at Rosses Point, Dixie Dean wowing the Mardyke, Milltown and Dalymount – because that is how it really was. And reflect on how his very presence brought colour and joy to so many in the tough times of 1930s Ireland.

Dixie Uncut – The Lost Interview is the player's life and times in his own words. Its very existence is a story in itself. In May 1971, the *Liverpool Echo* launched a serialised version of Dean's life that was originally intended to fill sports column inches over the quiet summer weeks between football seasons but that actually ended up running for an incredible four and a half months! The paper's editor at the time, Michael Charters, spent weeks with Dixie as he relived his glory days – the results of the conversations spilling out into the *Echo* day after day, gobbled up by an eager and attentive audience.

At the end of the run, the paper's library staff asked Charters for the original manuscripts, which they filed away in the *Echo's* archive. And there they lay, largely undisturbed, for over two decades – until they were rediscovered by one of Charters's successors, Ken Rogers, while he researched a book on Everton. Realising the value of the uncut manuscript, Rogers refiled it in a locked store beneath the *Echo* building that also saved for posterity historical sports pictures and handwritten statistical books compiled by the paper's sports writers spanning a century. Rogers believed that someday Dixie Dean's story would be retold.

Another 13 years passed, until an editorial meeting at the paper in 2005 noted that it was coming up to the 25th anniversary of Dean's death – the man who gave goalkeepers nightmares having suffered a fatal heart attack just after the final whistle of a Merseyside derby at Goodison Park in March 1980. Rogers's thoughts turned to the manuscript in the newspaper's vaults, and within a few months, the 450 pages of the 18-part series were released as a book to commemorate a quarter-century since the great Everton marksman's passing.

Sligo Rovers may only get a brief mention in the *Liverpool Echo's* interviews, but it's clear that Dean's time playing in Ireland and the warmth with which he was received meant a lot to him. The interviews also reveal much about the life of a footballer in England in the 1920s and 1930s, when clubs ruled the roost and players, no matter how great, were largely limited to a maximum wage of £8 a week (sterling). In today's money, we'd be talking around €515 weekly for a top gun like Dixie Dean.[1] Good money, for sure. But if the market were as open and favourable for players then as it is now, the sky would have been the limit in terms of earnings for a player of his calibre.

Put it this way: if Dean had played today, he'd certainly never have needed to go to Sligo to earn a crust. He could easily have retired and lived a life of luxury, maybe played at being a pundit for a bit or just spent his time on the golf course. Or if he had wanted to play on further into his 30s, he'd have had no end of offers from around the world. Major League Soccer in Los Angeles, maybe, or even the big-money attractions of China might well have been his last port of call. The League of Ireland and Sligo Rovers wouldn't have been a consideration.

But back in 1939, Irish clubs weren't constrained by the English league's wage cap – meaning that the offer of games in Ireland had to be seriously considered. There was money to be made. That said, the decision must not have been an easy one for Dean – as it meant

---

1   A note on the relative worth of money in this book: I've used the Inflation Calculator for Ireland on the Central Statistics Office website to convert sums from the 1930s into current (approximate) amounts. This involves converting sums into euro amounts first, then using the calculator, which tells you how much money you would require in a later period to purchase the same volume of consumer goods and services.

leaving his wife Ethel and his three little boys (Billy, Geoff and Ralph, who were six, five and four years of age, respectively) back in Nottingham for the duration. Not a sacrifice the modern player would have to contend with – even a run-of-the-mill Premier League squad player would have the financial wherewithal these days to move his family and more or less anyone else of his choosing to the city or town where he would be plying his trade.

But to underline just how limited the options were for players in Dean's time when their playing days were over, on his return to England in the summer of 1939 after his time with Sligo and on the eve of World War II, the only job he could pick up was at the abattoir in Birkenhead, where he remained until he was enlisted in the army in 1940.

Post-war, Dean went on to run a pub in Chester, the Dublin Packet, until 1961, ultimately returning to Merseyside to work four years as a security man before his retirement in 1965. A proud, honest and grounded man, Dixie felt no sense of entitlement and never lamented his lot – for him, all work to earn a crust was worthy. Once being an internationally revered football player conferred no extra rights on him in those difficult economic days.

And yet it's still hard to imagine a giant of the game in such circumstances when you see how the giants live now. And Dixie Dean truly was a giant. A legend.

His abilities and records should not be underestimated just because he played so long ago. If he were playing now, I'm quite certain he'd be spoken of in the same breath as Cristiano Ronaldo or Lionel Messi. And just imagine the hullabaloo if either of those two ended up togging out at the Showgrounds in Sligo for the Bit O' Red on a cold winter's Sunday! But it is that calibre of player that you should keep in the back of your mind as you read this book. Every time you see Dixie's name, think Ronaldo and hold that level of football greatness in your mind's eye. That is the reality of Dean's standing in the pantheon of football greats, and it's what gives this tale its storybook appeal.

2

'Offer Accepted,
Will be There Friday'

'OFFER ACCEPTED, will be there Friday.'

One can only imagine the impact of that six-word telegram in the town of Sligo, in Ireland's far west, when it was received on Tuesday, 24 January 1939.

Dixie Dean, one of the greatest footballers of his (or any other) generation, had agreed to come and play for little Sligo Rovers of the League of Ireland. Dixie Dean, a genuine football superstar. Dixie Dean, the greatest goal-getter in English football history, whose league record of 60 goals in the 1927/28 season has never since been troubled, let alone bested.

Dixie Dean was going way out west to the Bit O' Red, Sligo Rovers, a club that had only been playing senior football for five years, and to a small market town where the love of the game had been nurtured by the British soldiers who had been garrisoned there when Ireland was but a small part of a colonial empire.

Sligo was the very definition of a footballing outpost. Back in 1939, there were only two senior clubs operating in the west of the island of Ireland. Sligo Rovers was one, with Limerick, a little further south and based in another garrison town, being the other. Football in the Irish Free State, now 18 years young, was popular, but then, as now, clubs from Dublin tended to dominate the scene.

Had Dean been sending that telegram to one of them, to champions Shamrock Rovers, for instance, it would still have been a footballing sensation. But the idea that he would be going to live and play in Dublin would not have seemed anywhere as unlikely.

But it was Sligo Rovers, an ambitious club, yes, an increasingly successful club, yes, but a club in a humble, isolated market town of just 13,000 people. Hardly the most obvious destination for one of the game's greatest and most glorified exponents, even in the twilight of his career. And yet, he'd be there on Friday.

* * *

There's a wonderful fairy-tale element to William Ralph Dean's time in Ireland. Indeed, it's a heartwarming tale – akin in some ways to the plot of an Ealing comedy – in which everyone ultimately had happy memories, if not the ending all desired. But context is needed before we let our hearts run away with the story.

Because, let's face it, England's greatest-ever goalscorer wasn't coming to Irish football in his prime. If Dean was still at the height of his powers, the list of suitors would have been endless. Indeed, Sligo Rovers were not even suitors – not initially anyway, which given the striker's standing in the game is hardly a surprise.

But the reality is that the Irish opportunity arose just after Dean had seemingly hung up his boots for the last time – the hard yards and injuries of his 16 years as a professional having taken their toll. After 437 league and cup games since beginning his professional career with Tranmere Rovers, and 408 goals later, Dean had agreed to cancel his contract with Notts County of the English Division Three after just nine appearances in 18 frustrating, injury-dogged months at the club. His playing career over, Dean announced that he was going into the talent-scouting business.

But timing, even of the fortuitous variety, is often crucial in football. And so it was in this case. Just as Dean was contemplating his new future, over in Ireland the Sligo Rovers management committee was considering the second half of the 1938/39 season.

The Connacht club sat second in the table behind reigning champions Shamrock Rovers – but in truth, holding a comfortable lead over the chasing pack, the Dublin side were odds-on favourites to claim a second title in two seasons. For the Bit O' Red, all eyes were on the Football Association of Ireland (FAI) Cup – for some, the most glorious trophy in the game and one Sligo had never won – which was set to get underway in February. It was a competition that was sure to drive interest and revenue should Rovers find it in their power to mount a convincing assault in the winter and spring of 1939.

The club hierarchy felt that to hold on to the runners-up spot in the league and compete for the cup, more firepower would be required. And that is where Dean came in – not as a target, but as a talent-spotter who could find Sligo a striker from across the water to drive their cup ambitions.

* * *

The details of how the deal came about were a little sketchy in Dean's mind when he talked to the *Liverpool Echo*'s sports editor, Michael Charters, in 1971 about his life and times.

Dixie recounted that in the run-up to the move he had been struggling for fitness with Notts County, having broken a bone in his foot in only his second game. The nastiness of the injury saw him laid up in Nottingham Hospital for around two months, in which time it was decided that surgery would be needed to solve the problem. 'When I came out of hospital I was only hobbling about and only managed to play another seven games for Notts County altogether,' recalled Dean.

A little while later, having made his move into scouting, Dean says he received a letter from Sligo Rovers looking for his help in finding them a centre-forward. 'I asked one or two players and the first thing they said was, "Isn't it a bit dangerous out there with all this IRA lark going on?"'

The players were referring to a sabotage and bombing campaign being waged by the Irish Republican Army across 1938 and into 1939 aimed at customs outposts along the border on the partitioned island and that also stretched to targets in mainland Britain. Tensions were high, and so it was hardly surprising that going to play in Ireland wasn't an especially attractive proposition for some Englishmen at the time.

'So I couldn't find anybody who wanted to go to Ireland, and I told them so. Eventually, they cabled me to ask if I would play for them. By then I had got over my foot operation, and I was doing a bit of training. Notts County were prepared to let me go so I cabled back to Sligo and arranged to meet their officials in Dublin to discuss terms.'

The passage of time can play tricks on the mind and the memory. Dean's recall of how the deal came about some 30 years after the fact was a little at odds with the details he provided to another Liverpool paper back in 1939, just as the deal was being struck.

The following story from the *Liverpool Evening Express* was dated 27 January 1939, the day Dixie was due to arrive in Sligo. The first-hand report involving quotes attributed to the player himself and filed under the byline 'Pilotsports Log' provides a clearer picture of the events that saw Dean Sligo-bound. Interestingly, Sligo Rovers weren't the only club interested in bringing Dixie across the Irish Sea.

'Billy (Dixie) Dean, the famous England, Everton and Notts County centre-forward and football's greatest goal-getter, will today sign for Sligo, the League of Eire club, unless there is a last-minute hitch. Dean crossed to Ireland last night from Liverpool, and talked with the Sligo club officials today. If he signs, he will play for Sligo against Shelbourne on Sunday. Shelbourne were also anxious to sign Dean. About two weeks ago I announced that Dean's contract with Notts County had been cancelled by mutual consent, and that Dean would retire from active football and concentrate on talent-spotting.

'Well, his new job was the main cause of his return to football. Billy was living in Nottingham and spending a lot of time on the junior grounds. He had one or two likely players in mind when along came a message from Sligo asking if Dean could find them a centre-forward. They mentioned the terms they were prepared to offer. "I set about the job of finding them a centre-forward," said Billy when he came in to see me, and "I knew it was not going to be easy. I reflected on the offer, and then the thought came to me, well, if they want a centre-forward I wonder what terms they would offer me? I asked them, and apparently they liked the idea for they offered me terms which I could not possibly refuse. That is the sole reason why I'm off to Ireland." Now you know the real story why Billy Dean changed his mind. He goes to a fine team which has lacked only one faculty – scoring power. Well, he should remedy that.'

Dean's rather swift retirement U-turn suggests that perhaps he'd felt he'd been a little hasty in calling time on his playing career. Notts County had clearly lost faith in his ability to recover and perform – and in truth, given his rather sorry time at the club, it would have been hard to blame them. Dean had probably lost faith too – but then it may be that the break from playing afforded by his move into scouting had given his body valuable time to recuperate. He was, as after all, only 32 years of age.

Giving up the game is tough, however. Even those of us still toiling into our 40s in the weekly five-a-side and feeling Father Time's hot breath on the back of our necks know that. But more pertinent in this case was the fact that the future for retiring footballers of that era, even those of superstar status, wasn't anything like it is today.

Dean would still need to put food on his family's table and keep a roof over their heads. He would need to earn a wage. Scouting would provide an income, yes, but a potentially tenuous one. There were no guarantees. So feeling refreshed and maybe a touch trepidatious about the future, it was hardly surprising that the move to Ireland proved hard to resist. Good money in his pocket, the ball at his feet and a chance to prove to himself and others that he still had something to offer, Dixie boarded the boat to Dublin.

* * *

Divine intervention? We're on a Mission from God!

The Sligo Champion of Saturday, 28 January offered some further detail on the move.

> On Tuesday morning (January 24), Mr A. J. Donal, Hon. Secretary to Sligo Rovers received a telegram from Dean which said "Can you increase offer for personal services?" Previously, Dean had

refused Rovers' offer, but promised he would aid in securing a centre-forward for the team. The Management Committee met hurriedly and decided to wire another offer.

It was that offer that the former England and Everton star accepted. Sligo's committee must have been in a state of near disbelief when that telegram arrived. Yes, Dean had apparently hung up his boots. Yes, he'd struggled badly with injury in his time in Nottingham. But on the flip side, the legendary striker had nevertheless bagged 27 goals across 40 games in all competitions for the Everton only two seasons before!

From a purely football perspective, this was nothing less than a coup for Sligo Rovers. And then there was the financial angle. After all, even if Dean had to hop around on one leg, such was his profile, the Irish football public would still surely pay to see him play, even in unidextrous form![2]

Given the enormity of what they had pulled off, the club's committee members would have been forgiven for wondering if some greater power was at work. And as it happens, they may well have been right!

The Sligo Champion report on the contacts and negotiations that ultimately saw Dean go west mentioned

---

2   Note: I considered removing this quip on learning that later in life, in 1976 in fact, as his health declined, Dixie had to have his right leg amputated due to a blood clot. I certainly didn't want to appear insensitive to his suffering. However, on mentioning the line to his granddaughter Melanie Prentice, she told me that I shouldn't worry about it, as the idea of him hopping around the pitch but still pulling a crowd was 'actually something he'd have found quite funny'. I do hope that is the case.

that 'the move was worked through the influence of a friend connected with Everton' but offered no detail as to who that may have been. However, in a piece written by Leo Gray for the paper in 1980, it becomes clear that divine or perhaps just a clerical intervention in the form of two Catholic clergymen played a rather crucial role.

According to the piece, the Right Reverend Monsignor Pat Collins was based in Sligo at the time, and he and a colleague may have been influential in bringing Dean to Irish football.

Monsignor Collins told Gray, 'I had been based in Liverpool and, just like today, there was intense rivalry between Liverpool and Everton. People were either Liverpudlians or Evertonians, and as it happened, I supported Everton and went to their games every Saturday.

'I became friendly with all the players, particularly Dixie Dean, so I suppose it was natural that Rovers asked me to make contact with him when I returned to Sligo. By this stage, Dixie was playing with Notts County, and Rovers obviously felt they could persuade him to come to Sligo. Anyway, I contacted a friend of mine in Liverpool, a Fr. Sergeant, and he contacted Dixie. That was the initial contact, and the rest is history.'

The Catholic Church in Ireland at the time was notorious for its overbearing and intrusive nature, casting a foreboding shadow over all society. But this was one intervention, the Church as football agents and go-betweens, that the people of Sligo and all those who got to witness Dean's greatness up and down the country will have had little cause to complain about!

3

Ambitious Club and
Living Legend

NO MATTER how much football has changed between Dean's era and our own, one thing certainly hasn't – sentiment's place in the game. Much as football is wrapped up in memories, nostalgia, heroes and villains, when your usefulness to a club drops below a certain threshold – and regardless of whether that line is real or perceived – your time is by and large up.

And so it was for Dixie Dean. By the 1936/37 season, Dean's position as the main source of goals for the Toffees (Everton Football Club's nickname) was coming under threat. In January of that year, the club had paid a record fee of £6,500 (€420,000) to Burnley for the services of a young striker named Tommy Lawton. The youngster, who was also to become an Everton legend, was deployed at inside-left as Dean continued his centre-forward duties. But it soon became clear that Lawton had been earmarked as Dean's successor.

Dixie had finished the season with a decent haul of goals (27 in 40 league and cup games) but found that his relationship with club secretary Theo Kelly was becoming increasingly strained. The striker admitted that he just couldn't get on with the Everton official and had increasingly come to feel that Kelly was actively working behind the scenes to make trouble for him.

Other clubs sensed it too, and with Everton struggling to find a rhythm at the start of the 1937/38 season, Division One rivals Blackpool made a play for Dean's services.

Ironically, in the third match of the season, the two sides met in a game that was to hasten the end of Dean's Everton career. During the course of a bruising encounter, he took a heavy blow to the head that saw several of his teeth loosened – and loosened with them was his grip on his role in the club's first team. In typical fashion, Dixie completed the fixture – but as a result of the injury, he was left out of the side for the following match, with Lawton replacing him in the centre-forward berth. It was a role the promising youngster would retain for the rest of the season.

On recovering from his injuries, Dean found himself largely confined to the Everton second string, making only two more starts for the first 11.

Dean told the *Liverpool Echo*'s Michael Charters that Sir Lindsay Parkinson, Blackpool's chairman, subsequently asked him to join the Seasiders, making him a very tempting offer. When he told Everton chairman Will Cuff of what was on the table and asked him what he thought, he recounts being told, 'You are not going to leave Everton. You've got a job here for life.'

Cuff's words were to prove decidedly apocryphal. On 23 October 1937, William Ralph Dean played his 399th and last game for Everton's first team. And on 11 March 1938, he was gone – the football world shocked to read, after several statements from Everton that Dean would not be leaving, that the player had been transferred to Division Three Notts County for £3,000 (€194,000) – ironically, the same amount Everton had paid to Tranmere Rovers when bringing him to Goodison Park.

The local press was flabbergasted at the apparent about-turn by the club's hierarchy. And with Everton refusing to comment, the sports pages, apparently unwilling to incur the wrath of the club, reported that the transfer must have been agreed and conducted with the best interests of Dean at heart.

Dean saw it very differently. According to Nick Walsh, Dean alleged that 'Kelly had adopted an autocratic and disagreeable attitude to all the older players, particularly himself, and this he found to be intolerable, hence the decision to transfer.'

And so with his relationship with the club's main power broker on the floor and knowing that Football Association rules dictated that transfers would be restricted for the rest of the season after 16 March, Dean claimed that he was prepared to take the first decent offer that came along. It was that or see his situation at Everton deteriorate further.

'I was really fed up with the Everton set-up at that time, so I agreed to sign for [Notts] County – 13 years almost to the day after I had signed for Everton from Tranmere Rovers.'

An unceremonious end to his career at Goodison Park. Niggling injuries and a clash of personalities ushered Dean through the exit door. Sentiment was notable by its absence. A fact underlined by the behaviour of Kelly on the day Dean signed for County. According to the player himself, the Everton secretary was the only club official present at the signing, and he left without so much as a goodbye when the deed was done.

* * *

Sligo Rovers Football Club was established in September 1928, just a few months after Dean's most prolific season on Merseyside. The club, the result of the amalgamation of two junior soccer sides, Sligo Town and Sligo Blues, spent the first six seasons of its existence in junior football, initially in Connacht, before moving through the Dublin-based Sunday Alliance League and the Leinster Senior League before being elected to the Free State League (League of Ireland) in the summer of 1934.

Rovers adapted to senior football well, and in their first season, they finished a more than creditable third, just eight points behind champions Dolphin, a Dublin inner-city side who disappeared from the league only two years later. The season was also notable from a Sligo point of view for a strong and lucrative run in the FAI Cup.

But the westerners were ultimately to have their hearts broken at the penultimate stage, losing 2-0 to Dundalk in the semi-final.

The following term, the Bit O' Red suffered a touch of second-season syndrome, finishing well off the pace – eighth of the 12 league sides – and suffering a second-round exit from the FAI Cup at the feet of Drumcondra after a hard-fought replay. A disappointing return after the promise shown in their debut season in the top flight, but nevertheless, the club and its fans could definitely feel that they had established themselves in the league. And unsurprisingly, given the strong foundations that had been laid, success was not to be too long in coming.

Sligo Rovers began the 1936/37 season in blistering fashion, winning their first 11 league fixtures and blowing away their opposition. A dip in form in the second half of their league campaign that saw them win only five of their last 11 fixtures wasn't enough to stop them from running away with their first League of Ireland title. In fact, they won at a canter, ten points clear of Dundalk and crossing the finishing line with two league games to spare.

Top of the pile for the first time in their short history, and only the second club outside of Dublin to have won the league, Sligo Rovers were now clearly a force to be reckoned with in the Irish game.

But what glamour and wealth there was in Irish football at the time, which was drawing good crowds and was faring well against the rival sports of Gaelic football, hurling and rugby, certainly wasn't to be found on Ireland's western seaboard.

Competing with the big Dublin clubs, who had won 14 of the first 16 editions of the league since its inception in 1921 and who could command much bigger attendances in the capital, was never going to be easy. Taking the battle consistently to the likes of Shamrock Rovers and Bohemians, who had won ten titles between them, while based in a town whose population of just 13,000 souls was similar to the kinds of attendances the two Dublin giants would enjoy regularly, was a very tough ask.

That said, with no League of Ireland clubs in the rest of Connacht, nor in bordering County Donegal, Sligo Rovers did have the potential to draw on strong support from further afield – as Dean's arrival was to prove 18 months later.

Nevertheless, it was hardly a surprise when Shamrock Rovers took the league title back to Dublin in the 1937/38 season. The Bit O' Red would always have expected a strong response from the capital's big boys. What was disappointing for the supporters of the men from the west was the sloppy manner in which they relinquished their crown, failing to recover from a poor start to the campaign to finish in an uncompetitive sixth spot. And there was to be no solace or excitement drawn from the FAI Cup either, as Rovers exited after a first-round replay with the other garrison powerhouse, Dundalk, who were now becoming something of a bogey side for the Sligo club.

The 1938/39 Shield competition gave Sligo fans a taste of just what they might expect in the league that term.

The Shield was considered the third most prestigious of the prizes on offer in Irish football. It was played from August to November, ahead of the league season, and involved a game against each of your league opponents. For Sligo Rovers, this meant six home fixtures, with five away.

The five draws that ultimately derailed their Shield ambitions were a portent of the league season to come. Rovers, playing slick and entertaining football – a brand for which they were to become synonymous – proved unable, time and again, to put opponents away. Unfortunately, their unconvincing Shield form was carried into their League of Ireland fixtures. Three draws and two defeats in their first ten games left them with too big a gap to bridge on defending champions Shamrock Rovers by the halfway point of the season. But better times and huge excitement were just around the corner for the fans of the Connacht club.

* * *

Back in the 1927/28 season when Dean scored 60 times to set the record for the most goals scored in a single English league season, he was just 21. And while he would never match that tally again, the goals did flow with a consistency and volume across his career that marked him as a striker apart.

Dixie was still a teen when he left his first professional club, Tranmere Rovers, for Goodison Park in 1925.

During his 13-year career with the Toffees, he won the Division One championship on two occasions and captained Everton to their first FA Cup win in 1933, scoring in a 3-0 win over Manchester City. It was said at the time that his mere presence on the team sheet could add 5,000 to a Goodison Park attendance.

That pulling power wasn't without controversy at times, as Nick Walsh pointed out. 'Some people suspected that when Dean was injured and could not play, announcements were often made to include his name in the side in order to deliberately induce more spectators to attend the match. It was reasonable to assume that many fans only made the effort to go to a game when they knew Dean would be playing, because attendances most certainly fell whenever he was absent.'

Dean scored 349 goals in 399 league matches for the Blues, plus a further 28 in 33 FA Cup ties and 18 in 16 games for England.

His tally certainly bears comparison with the very greatest goal-getters the game has produced. No one in English football history has come close to matching his 60 goals in a single top-flight season. Tom 'Pongo' Waring[3] of Aston Villa came closest with a 49-goal total in 1930/31, but he was still 11 goals shy of Dean's record. The great Jimmy Greaves only got within 23 goals of Dean's total in his most plentiful of seasons with Spurs in 1962/63, while prolific scorers such as Gary Lineker and Ian Rush – two of the deadliest strikers in front of goal

---

3 Waring was born only three months before Dean and also hailed from Birkenhead. Like Dixie, he also cut his predatory teeth with Tranmere Rovers.

in my youth – were 30 and 28 goals short, respectively, in their best seasons.

And when you look at the much-vaunted strikers of the Premier League era, the record 34-goal hauls of Andrew Cole and Alan Shearer in the 42-game seasons of 1993/94 and 1994/95 were short by a considerable distance. Put simply, Dixie Dean scored in one season what the greats that were to follow him struggled and strained to score in two!

Even when you compare Dean's record with attacking legends across the continent, the Everton man's tally shows why he should be seated at the top table when any history of the game is written.

Der Bomber, Gerd Müller of Germany and Bayern Munich, notched 398 goals in 453 league, cup and European games for his club (a rate of 1.13 goals per game, compared with Dixie's 1.14) and an incredible 68 in 62 internationals for his country. But despite Müller's eye for goal, his best return in a league season was 40 in 1971/72. To be fair to the German marksman, he scored those 40 in a 34-game Bundesliga season. Had he eight more games to play, could he have bagged another 20 goals to match Dixie's effort? Being kind, let's just say it'd be unlikely!

So what about the two greatest goalscorers in European and world football of the last decade or more, Lionel Messi and Cristiano Ronaldo? How do they compare?

Well, although the two have scored at a consistently eye-watering rate throughout their careers, their best efforts, in 38-game La Liga seasons – 50 for the Argentinian in 2011/12 and 48 for the Portuguese in 2014/15 – are the closest we've seen in the modern game. But they still fall short. Undoubtedly, both would have come much closer had they an additional four league games to play in their most prolific domestic seasons. But scoring the ten and 12 goals, respectively, they'd have required to just match the Englishman still seems improbable.

Comparing players from different eras is a largely fruitless activity, of course. There are so many variables at play – the quality of their team-mates and the quality of their opposition, for example. The manner in which the rules were applied across eras is also a factor. The strikers of today are a much more protected species, after all. And they get to play on pitches of such fine quality that Dean would have been agog. How many goals would Dixie have scored in the modern era in such conditions and with today's footballs and boots? And by the same token, how would Messi and Ronaldo have fared in the mud, sand and straw of an English winter and in the sights of the less constrained, indeed less restrained, 1930s defender?

None of this is to say that Dean was better than any of the players listed. But as *Liverpool Echo* journalist and Everton historian David Prentice put it to me, 'All you can say with any certainty was that William Ralph "Dixie" Dean was the best of his generation by an absolute mile.'

* * *

Dean was probably best known for his prowess in the air as a player. But his ability to strike a ball with power and accuracy off either foot and his creativity and reading of the game – all of which shone at Sligo Rovers as they did in England – shouldn't be underestimated.

Matt Busby, who played in the 1933 FA Cup Final for Manchester City against Dean's Everton, wrote of the fabled centre-forward in his book *Soccer at the Top: My Life in Football* that it was both 'a delight and a nightmare' to be pitted against him.

'He was the perfect specimen of an athlete, beautifully proportioned, with immense strength, adept on the ground but with extraordinary skill in the air. However close you watched him, his timing in the air was such that he was coming down before you got anywhere near him, and he hit the ball with his head as hard and accurately as most players could kick it. Defences were close to panic when corners came over. And though he scored a huge tally of goals with headers, he was an incredibly unselfish and amazingly accurate layer-off of chances for others … He would out-jump, out-time, out-head any defender or any number they could pack into the area.'

Dean's former team-mate at Everton, and later manager of England, Joe Mercer, was similarly effusive. 'Dixie was unique, probably the greatest scoring machine the game has ever known, or ever will know. He hadn't a negative thought in his head; he never showed any nerves or any tension, he always believed his team would win and he never, never stopped scoring goals. In the air, he could achieve anything and everything – gliding, deflecting, nodding it down or, as he did mostly, scoring. On the ground he had two good feet, never needed a backlift and would regularly poke in goals with a toe end. Most of all he was a terrific competitor, perfect for the job in physique and temperament.

'What is forgotten is that his scoring feats had a potent influence on the game. Every opposing team had to wrestle with the problem of how to stop Dixie but very few succeeded. It has been said that as many as four or five defenders were deputed to check him yet all they succeeded in doing was to watch him win the ball in the air and direct it to one or other of his capable colleagues.

'He was a flamboyant personality and made every match a big occasion. He was good with the public and marvellous with kids, and, on top of all this, a great captain.'

Not a bad reference that.

It's clear that Dean played the game in a very different environment to that of today. Any available footage suggests a much more bruising experience, although match reports of the time do talk of high levels of artistry.

Dixie's aerial mastery was a major weapon in a time when conditions underfoot could often range from treacherous to unplayable across the English winter and spring. His incredible timing, his prodigious leap (Dean would often entertain the public on nights out by jumping from a standing position on to the surface of a snooker table!) and absolute control of the football with his head were rightly legendary.

And we are not talking of the plastic-coated, light, player-friendly balls of modern times. To head a ball in the 1930s, especially on a wet day, was a very risky enterprise. The weight alone left many seeing stars, while the laces that held the leather together could also do damage. And this is not to mention leaping and jumping whilst wearing football boots that would have proven just as useful on a construction site!

But Dean was a player apart. He was born to score goals – something he did prolifically from his days as a schoolboy in Birkenhead and Merseyside right to his last professional games in Ireland.

'I was always mad about playing football,' Dean said in *Dixie Uncut*. His childhood memories were dominated by the game and his early love of Everton. It was all-consuming. 'I was so keen,' he said, 'that I used to go and train by myself.'

And it was that love of the game, a passionate affair that began in childhood, that explains quite a bit about how Dean developed into the player he was.

Anyone who has kids knows there are two groups when it comes to playing football. There are those who need to be encouraged to go out and play – more so in these days when the games console can exert an iron grip. And then there are those who don't need any encouragement at all, those whose first waking thought is to grab a ball and play, those who have to be dragged in from playing football when the evening draws in.

Dean was very much in the latter camp – and if he couldn't find anyone to play with, he'd play and practise

– relentlessly – by himself. His own accounts of how he learned the basics and honed his skills will resonate with anyone who has kids with that same level of interest.

'There was an old chapel in the north end of Birkenhead, and I used to kick a ball against the chapel wall and keep running up and down playing the ball backwards and forwards against the wall,' Dean recalled of his own 'training sessions'.

'But one of the greatest things I can remember was the chapel roof. It helped to give me a good start with the old heading trick. I chalked the outline of a goal on the chapel wall and then threw the ball on to the roof.

'I'd wait for it to come down and then I'd move in to head it against the wall between the goal posts. Looking back, I'm sure this helped me with my heading, but I must say that I was good at heading. It was a natural gift.'

A thought: with attendance levels falling at churches in modern times, perhaps opening their grounds to some impromptu football training might get the kids flooding back to God! No, maybe not.

Anyway, Dean simply couldn't get enough of the game or of scoring goals. And despite all that he had achieved in his career, it was clear in his interview with Charters for the *Liverpool Echo* series that the day that he scored 18 goals across three matches as a schoolboy still meant a lot to him.

'I was 13 at the time. There was a Birkenhead Boys trial at Prenton Playing Fields in the morning starting about nine o'clock. I scored six in the match and then me and the rest of the lads in the team got on our bikes and dashed down to Birkenhead Park to play another match starting at eleven o'clock.

'I scored another six goals for them and then in the afternoon I played for another team called Melville and scored another six!

'So that was 18 in three games, so I wasn't surprised when I got 60 in a season for Everton. I always had a lust for goals … but I practised hard at it.'

Leaving school at 14, Dean got a job with his father on the Wirral Railways as an apprentice fitter. 'I left school on Friday and started work the following Monday,' he recalled. Dixie used to take the night shift, as it gave him more opportunity to play football – quickly establishing himself as centre-forward for the works team.

Perhaps, unsurprisingly, one team wasn't really enough to satisfy his burning desire to just play and score, so Dean also turned out for local side Pensby United in the Wirral Combination League. And it was here that he came to the attention of the professional game in the form of Division Three Tranmere Rovers who offered him his first professional contract in the summer of 1923 at the tender age of 16.

Dean made his debut for the reserves in September of that year, and while his performances saw him make his full debut and two other appearances in the first team that season, he lined out mainly in the club's reserves. However, a dreadful injury in which he lost a testicle (yes, a testicle) in a Cheshire Senior Cup tie saw his season finish early and actually threatened to put a stop to his professional career almost before it had properly started.

But showing the powers of recovery and the fortitude that saw him come back time and again from bad injuries, Dean returned the following season and really began to make his mark.

The young centre-forward became a regular for Tranmere during the 1924/25 season in Division Three North and immediately began making a name for himself. Dean bagged an eye-catching 27 goals in 27 league games for the Prenton Park outfit that term, a feat made all the more impressive given his side finished second bottom that campaign, amassing only 59 goals in total!

And those prodigious and prolific efforts didn't go unnoticed. First Newcastle United, then Aston Villa, then Arsenal came calling – but Dean said no. 'You see, I was just waiting for one club to come for me and that was Everton.'

Dixie got his dearest wish on 16 March 1925, when he signed for the Toffees for £3,000 (€194,000), a record fee for a player from Division Three and for an 18-year-old at the time. He saw the season out with Tranmere Rovers before going straight into Everton's first-team squad in preparation for the 1926/27 season. And it is fair to say, he never looked back.

4

The 60-Goal Season

'I always had a lust for goals.'

Dixie Dean

FOR ALL the great achievements of William Ralph 'Dixie' Dean, the 60-goal league season of 1927/28 is perhaps the greatest testament to his prodigious talent. It was the extreme manifestation of his desire for goals, his skill and his cast-iron constitution, and it gave him a fame that was to last a lifetime.

Over 90 years later, and with all the wonderful striking talent that has been produced by or drawn to the English game in that time, it's fair to say it's a record that will never be matched, let alone mastered.

But although we may marvel at the number 60, or struggle to comprehend how it could have been achieved, the figure itself doesn't quite convey the outrageous drama of that season, particularly in the latter stages, for

Dean, Everton and football itself. At the risk of sounding clichéd, a Hollywood scriptwriter would've been ordered to have a rethink had it been the plot for a movie.

Dean had set the groundwork with a truly scintillating first half of the season. As the referee called time on the Boxing Day clash with title rivals Cardiff City, the 21st game of the league campaign, the Everton forward had once again been in clinical form. The Toffees had won the encounter by two goals to one in front of more than 50,000 hardy souls at a frigid Goodison Park. Dean, the Toffees hero, scored both goals in a display described uniformly as brilliant across the newspapers. He had now amassed 33 goals as the teams turned for home.

With another 21 games to play, Dean needed just six more goals to see the Everton record books rewritten. D.B. Freeman's club record of 38 in a league season, which had been set 19 years previously, would surely be broken. Indeed, such was the Birkenhead boy's insatiable appetite that the existing Division One record of 43 set by Blackburn Rovers' Ted Harper in 1925/26 also looked to be on borrowed time.

The Everton man had scored in 16 of his side's games up to and including the Cardiff City clash. His tally included seven braces, three hat-tricks and five against a bewildered Manchester United. Dean had actually only figured in 20 of the Goodison men's fixtures – missing a 7-0 destruction of West Ham in late October (he was away on England duty). One can only wonder at how many he might have scored that day given such generous opposition. No matter, he was scoring with such regularity that records looked certain to fall.

Well, maybe all except for one – the towering 59-goal haul of Middlesbrough's George Camsell, achieved the previous season.

* * *

Spare a thought for George, Boro's record goalscorer. For if it wasn't for Dixie Dean, you'd probably have heard and read more about the Middlesbrough legend and his goalscoring feat of the 1926/27 English Division Two season. That term, the 24-year-old centre-forward didn't just break the record for goals scored in a single English league campaign, he obliterated it.

Prior to Camsell's fantastic total, the record belonged to James Cookson of Chesterfield, who had bagged 44 goals in Division Three North the previous term.

Camsell, who had arrived at Ayresome Park that same year but had managed only four appearances for the club's first 11, began his record-breaking season still in the Boro reserves, watching from the sidelines as his side scored just once in their first four league outings. However, his chance came in game five when an injury to first-choice centre-forward Jimmy McClelland saw George given a start against Hull.

Unpromisingly, he drew a blank, offering little or no evidence of the deluge to come. The following weekend, however, Camsell's incredible scoring sequence began. A brace at home to Bradford lit the fuse on an incredible six months for the Durham-born attacker as he set off on a blistering run that saw him score another 43 goals in just 23 games, surpassing Cookson's record by late February! Camsell's scoring rate did take something of a dip after reaching that mark. In relative terms anyway, as he banged in another 16 in the closing months of the season to reach the eye-watering mark of 59 goals in 37 league appearances.

His total was part of a very busy set of seasons for the era's football statisticians when scoring records were set and reset in quick succession. Cookson's 44-goal tally had come just a season after that of Darlington's David Brown, who had notched 39 goals in 1924/25, in turn eclipsing the previous record of 38 jointly held by Joe Smith of Bolton Wanderers (1920/21) and the aforementioned Freeman of Everton (1908/09).

The leap in goal returns achieved by Cookson and then Camsell was seen by many as a by-product of a change in the offside rule before the 1925/26 season. The rule change involved reducing the number of defenders from three to two who needed to be positioned between an attacking player and the goal for them not to be deemed offside. That adjustment saw the average number of goals scored per game across England's four divisions rise from 2.45 in September 1924 to 3.6 a year later. A number of forward players made hay in this period as teams desperately sought to find ways to combat a rule that was clearly in favour of attacking play.

However, it'd be unfair to suggest that the rule change solely explains Camsell's feat – or that of Dean, which was to follow a season later. Clearly, their ability to read the game and how it had changed allied with that innate gift of all great strikers of being in the right place at the right time were central to their achievements – but goalscoring is about so much more. It's one thing to be there, after all, but it's quite another to stick the ball in the back of the net at rates that went way beyond the merely prolific! The rule change was there to be exploited by all, but Camsell and Dean did so with a ruthlessness that was unparalleled.

The Times noted as much the day after Camsell topped Cookson's record in February 1927: 'The new offside rule has, of course, made scoring a good deal easier than formerly but Camsell's feat is a remarkable one … It is a common belief that something more than skill is required today, that strong physical power must be added to craft. But while football is a game for the strong man, skill still has its reward, as has been seen in the case of Middlesbrough. Not only has Camsell created a new "record" but the team as a whole promise to obtain more goals this season than have ever before been gained. Their football has always been a delight, and in these days when force threatens to take the place of craft, it is good that they should have been so handsomely rewarded.' And indeed they were. Boro went on to win Division Two at a canter, amassing an impressive 122 league goals as they did so.

The English game's second tier it may have been, but the football world was nevertheless agog. On the last day of the season, when Camsell netted his side's only goal in a 1-0 win at Swansea, *The Guardian*'s reporter wrote that this was a record 'that may stand for all time'. He had every reason to think so – with young George breaking the previous record by 16 goals. But he hadn't counted on the emergence of Dixie Dean who was to reduce Camsell's efforts to largely footnote status the following May.

* * *

While the Middlesbrough centre-forward was setting Division Two alight in the autumn of 1926, Dixie Dean was only just returning to the field of play with Everton after a serious motorcycle accident that summer. Having only started playing in October, Dean finished the season, only his second in blue, with 21 league goals in 27 games. It was an impressive performance considering how close he had come to never appearing on a football field again.

The previous June, Dean had been on his motorbike with a female acquaintance riding pillion, taking a jaunt towards North Wales. According to Nick Walsh's Dean biography, newspaper reports told of how a motorcycle sidecar that had been weaving in and out of the oncoming traffic slammed into the Everton star's bike, hurling Dean and his passenger into the road.[4] The footballer and the two occupants of the motorcycle combination

---

4   According to Walsh, Dixie claimed he remembered nothing after the incident, which is more than understandable. Oddly, however, in *Dixie Uncut*, Dean tells a different story in terms of the accident itself, recounting that an oncoming car on the wrong side of the road gave him two options – to plough into said vehicle or run off the road and down a mountainside. In a split-second decision, he pushed his passenger to safety and then hurtled through the car's windscreen. The result ultimately was the same, although the reason for the disparity remains unclear.

were picked up unconscious and taken on the back of a truck to Lluesty Infirmary near Holywell in Flintshire. Dixie's passenger was taken by car to the same location, but having thankfully suffered just a broken ankle, she was discharged the following day.

Dean, however, wasn't quite so fortunate. 'I fractured my skull, broke a cheekbone and fractured my jaw in two places,' he recalled in *Dixie Uncut*.

Dixie was unconscious for 36 hours, and as the infirmary where he was being cared for didn't have X-ray equipment, it was over a week before he could be moved to a hospital in Liverpool and a full diagnosis of his injuries completed. The Everton club doctor, Dr James Baxter, was deeply worried after several visits to check on Dean and feared that his career could well be over at the tender age of 19.

Surgical intervention was required, with metal plates being inserted in his jaw to aid in its healing. Dean spent several months in hospital and then in a nursing home convalescing before making his comeback for Everton's reserves at Huddersfield in early October. According to the man himself, a special trainload of fans travelled from Liverpool to see the game, as it was feared it might very well be his last. The Everton staff were worried that heading the heavy ball could be too much now for their centre-forward. But there was really only one way to find out. So according to Dean, outside-right Teddy Critchley was told to get a cross in for him to attack as early in the game as possible to test not just his physical recovery but his nerve as well.

'I remember it was a very heavy day,' said Dean, 'so naturally we were all worried about what was going to happen when I headed the ball.' Dixie was told to come off immediately if he felt any pain or discomfort. 'After about a quarter of an hour, over came the ball from Teddy Critchley. I thought to myself, "Here goes", and I went up to head it. The ball flew into the net.'

Dean claimed he never felt any ill effects from the injury. Indeed, he believed that it may well have benefited his career! 'As a matter of fact, I think the skull fracture knitted twice as hard, and it considerably helped me with the old heading trick!' Whether there was any truth in that is very hard to say. But there certainly was nothing in the rumour among some fans at the time that plates had been left fused to Dean's skull that served only to strengthen the power of his headers!

What was not in question, however, was the depth of Dean's fortitude. It was an incident that would have put paid to many a man and, given the era and the fact that the heavy football of the 1930s was often enough to concuss a player even when it hadn't sapped up moisture, returning to play was no trifling matter. An inch either way on that June Sunday could have ended not just Dixie's career, but his life.

Had the worst happened, then George Camsell of Middlesbrough Football Club would still be revered as the record holder for the most goals scored by an individual player in an English league season.

And Dixie Dean would have been a sad footnote in the game's history, a wonderful talent lost to an accident before he could fulfil his burgeoning potential.

* * *

Such were the demands of the era that the afternoon after their Boxing Day clash with Cardiff City, Everton were in action again in the return fixture against their Welsh rivals. However, the Bluebirds got their revenge on a raw day at Ninian Park, taming Dean and his colleagues in an impressive 2-0 triumph. It was only the fifth time that season that the Everton striker had failed to register a goal.

Four days later, however, Dixie made up for the blip, claiming yet another brace against Sheffield Wednesday, his ninth of the season. Everton ran out 2-1 winners, the victory giving them a four-point gap at the top of the table heading into the new year. Dixie had now scored 35 times that season alone, and a remarkable 93 in his 94 Everton league appearances since his debut for the club in March 1925! And he was still a few days shy of celebrating his 21st birthday.

Meanwhile, the Division One race was simmering nicely in the cold of the English winter. Everton, in search of their third title and their first since 1915, had daylight between themselves and a tightly packed group of chasers. Only a couple of points separated Cardiff, Huddersfield Town, Newcastle United, Leicester City and Tottenham Hotspur, all of whom could boast genuine title aspirations.

Dean's prodigious scoring was also grabbing the attention of football fans up and down the country as the records of Freeman, Smith and Harper came into view. Going into the new year, Dixie was just three goals shy of Freeman's Everton club record, but braces ten and 11 against Blackburn Rovers (in a 4-2 defeat for the Toffees) and George Camsell's Middlesbrough (in a 3-1 win at Goodison) saw that tally eclipsed.

Next in the centre-forward's sights was Harper's 43-goal Division One record. And with 17 games left, there seemed little doubt that the Blackburn player's marker would also soon be bested. But then a miserable February and March for Everton served to threaten their title pretensions, end their hopes of a historic double and put the brakes somewhat on Dean's scoring rate. The Toffees failed to win any of their next nine league fixtures and were knocked out of the FA Cup by Arsenal.

A 2-2 draw with Birmingham City in which a heavily policed Dean was kept off the score sheet was followed by their cup exit at Highbury.

The following weekend resulted in yet more pain as Everton gave ground to title challengers Huddersfield Town, who had famously won three titles in succession between 1924 and 1926 and were one of the giants of the English game at the time. A crowd of 51,000 paid into Leeds Road to watch what was a highly anticipated summit meeting and a game won comfortably four goals to one by the Terriers as Everton's mid-season wobble took hold. Dixie did score the Everton goal, to move on to 40 for the season, but there was little other cause for cheer.

And things went quickly from bad to worse for the Blues, crashing as they did to a shock 5-2 home defeat to Spurs the following Saturday, surrendering top spot in the league as a result. This time there was no consolation at all for Dean.

But there was little or no time for them to wallow in their misfortune, especially when their next game was a 25 February encounter with Liverpool at Anfield. The derby was a thriller, described by the *Liverpool Echo* the next day as 'The Best Derby Ever', with the sides sharing six goals. And it was especially thrilling for Dixie, as his hat-trick, his fifth of the season, saw him draw level with Harper and even receive the acclaim of the Kop, the rarest of rare occurrences for an Evertonian even to this day.

'Nothing pleased him more than to register goals against the Reds,' wrote Walsh. 'He made his usual acknowledgements to the Kop, bowing gracefully in the manner of a Spanish matador, following each of the goals he scored. The response would normally not be enthusiastic, but the "Kopites", although strongly partisan, are nothing if not appreciative of football achievement and when Dean equalled the Division One goalscoring record in that memorable game, they expressed their admiration no less than the other 50,000 spectators.'

The record equalled, Dean now had 13 games in which to set a new one. But with Camsell's English league record standing at 59 goals, there was little expectation that that tally would be or even could be beaten. The more so as Everton were continuing to struggle.

Dixie failed to register a goal in his next three games – a 0-0 draw with West Ham and two 1-0 defeats inflicted by Manchester United and Leicester City. Those results appeared to have put paid to Everton's title aspirations. Their poor run of form had seen them fall four points behind leaders Huddersfield – a considerable gap in an era where teams only received two points for a win.

Another scoreless draw was to follow against Portsmouth, although Dean was not involved in this one. Bizarrely, with the league race entering the finishing straight, he was away on English League duty, scoring twice in a 6-2 win against their Scottish counterparts!

How Everton must have rued their centre-forward's league selection and how they would have loved if his customary brace had been for them. Thankfully, their talisman returned for their next match, at home to Derby County, where he duly reminded his team-mates just what they'd missed. Two more goals for Dean, albeit with another point dropped by Everton.

The goals set a memorable landmark for Dean, however, as he finally put Harper's Division One record in the shade, moving on to 45 goals for the season. But March had been a disaster for Everton, and at that point, Dixie would surely have been willing to forgo the record if it meant a return to form for his struggling side.

Eight league games remained for the Blues to revive their championship hopes. But Dean was only going to figure in seven. He was set to miss Everton's next fixture at Roker Park against Sunderland – this time the England shirt beckoned and a clash with Scotland at Wembley. Happily for Everton, a 2-0 win over the Mackems put a stop to the rot. But for Dean, there was embarrassment, as he and his England colleagues were booed off the Wembley turf after suffering a historic 5-1 pasting by the Scots!

Odd as it may seem to say it, but it was really only on Dean's return to Goodison Park for the run-in that the real drama of that incredible season played out. Everton were still in the title race, with seven games remaining, while Dean, on his own campaign to set a new Division One goalscoring record, would have been confident of pushing the 50-goal mark. However, if thoughts of beating Camsell's 59-goal tally did cross his mind, they were likely given short shrift. After all, he'd have needed 14 goals in seven games just to equal the record, and 15 to beat it. Surely it could not be done. And anyway, with Everton still hoping to claim the league title, his focus needed to be on that collective goal, rather than any further personal glory.

Obviously, we know that he did the unthinkable – but even from this remove and with that knowledge, the run of goals he required at that point still makes his achievement almost other-worldly.

Nick Walsh describes those last seven games thus:

'What a sensational episode it produced, something so dramatic, it tended to arouse suspicions that it had all been deliberately staged! A colossal and stupendous epic, to coin the then Hollywood film preview ballyhoo indulgences of the time. Almost as many people watched football as they did cinema, but no rehearsals could be staged for soccer games, and no one could foresee at that time what was to come.'

The first of the seven fixtures drew 60,000 fans to Goodison Park to witness a comfortable 4-1 Everton win over Blackburn Rovers. Dean scored his almost customary brace on that Good Friday to move his tally up to 47. The result left the Toffees just a point behind Huddersfield. The following day, Saturday, 7 April, Dixie was at it again, scoring the equaliser eight minutes from time (goal 48) in a bruising encounter with Bury.

A solitary point wasn't exactly what the Blues had in mind, but they were buoyed with the news that neighbours Liverpool had beaten the Terriers that same afternoon, allowing Everton to go top on goal difference with five games to play. That said, with three games in hand, the Yorkshire side were still heavily favoured to be crowned champions.

It's amazing to look back at football in that era and think of players engaged in a double bill over two days as was required that Easter. And you'd imagine that in such circumstances, with personnel feeling the effects of a long season, they'd be given a few days off to recover. But you'd be wrong! Incredibly, the Everton hierarchy had different plans for Easter Monday. A trip to Dublin for a friendly against a Leinster Football Association selection was the reward for their hard-worked players! Indeed, the team had set sail on the Saturday evening, not long after their Bury stalemate.

Unsurprisingly, money was at the heart of the affair. Everton had agreed to the game on the understanding that they would receive £300 (€22,000) and half of any gate over £600 (€44,000) to grace Dalymount Park on the day.

As it happened, the matchup did create quite a bit of interest in Dublin, where, according to the *Irish Independent*, the fixture drew a gate of close to 40,000 and receipts of £900 (€66,000). Irish football enthusiasts were used to weekly updates in their papers on the exploits of the big clubs and stars across the water. And many had clearly been following the prolific goalscoring fortunes of Dean, the rising star of the English game.

'Those who paid the high prices witnessed a neat, if somewhat leisurely, display of the finer side of soccer,' reported the Irish daily. 'The result was a victory for Everton by 3-2. It could be said that there was nothing unusually brilliant about the play of Everton, but the international Dixie Dean supplied many flashes of great play that pleased the big crowd.'

Whatever the sense of the trip across the Irish Sea, Dixie didn't seem to have been unduly affected, for in the next league game the following Saturday, he brought up his half-century. The 3-1 win at Bramall Lane over Sheffield United included Dean's 13th brace of the campaign. With 50 goals in 35 games, the Everton man had already beaten Ted Harper's record by seven, and there were still four games left to play in which to raise the Division One scoring bar yet further.

Everton's 39th game of the season came midweek against reigning champions Newcastle United. A convincing 3-0 win saw their charge for the finish line pick up pace. Dixie was amongst the goalscorers, of course, notching goal 51 of his incredible crusade.

The Toffees now sat proudly on top of the table knowing the fate of the Division One title was in their own hands.

Aston Villa were next to visit Merseyside and suffer the wrath of a Dean-inspired home side. The 4-2 scoreline rather flattered the visitors, as Dean added two more to his tally, moving on to a brilliant 53 for the season.

But if the final games of the campaign were proving dramatic and breathless and Dean's achievements in front of goal leaving mouths agape, game 41 saw the whole story flip into overdrive. Turf Moor was the venue for an extraordinary affair where providence first offered hope that George Camsell's amazing record might not be entirely out of Dean's reach, before appearing to snatch it away again.

Everton won a ding-dong encounter 5-3, with Dixie producing a first-half display, and a four-goal salvo, that left all watching in awe. He was simply unplayable. And with 57 goals now to his name, many at the ground believed he might just blow Camsell's record away in the second period. But then disaster appeared to strike. Dean picked up a thigh strain that left him little more than a passenger in the second 45, and surely, surely, any hope of surpassing the Boro man's tally had been extinguished.

Given Dixie's extraordinary run of form, the idea of him scoring twice to equal Camsell's record in Everton's last game of the season couldn't be discounted – and a hat-trick to beat it, though unlikely, was doable. But he had to be fit and firing on all cylinders. And with just a week in which to recover, there was serious cause for doubt that he'd even be available – his thigh injury threatening to see him sidelined rather than face a date with destiny.

With the clock ticking and the situation looking decidedly grim, an unlikely hero, Harry Cooke, the Everton trainer, enters our story.

Cooke, a hugely popular figure in the Everton set-up and essentially the club's physio, had a week to work some magic and get Dean on the Goodison Park pitch the following Saturday. And he was determined to do absolutely everything in his power to give his idol a shot at immortality. Incredibly, Cooke's solution was to take up residence with Dixie for the entire week, applying treatment day and night to get him right.

'If it hadn't been for old Harry Cooke, I wouldn't have played at all,' Dean revealed in *Dixie Uncut*. 'Harry was really worried that I wouldn't be able to play against Arsenal, so when we got back from Burnley that night, he came with me to my home in Alderley Avenue, Birkenhead. He wanted to put hot plasters on my leg to get the muscle right.

'You're supposed to leave these plasters on pretty hot for about ten or twelve hours, but Harry wasn't content with that. He wanted to change them every two hours so that the heat from the plasters would really work.

'So, I went to bed, and he sat in a chair in my bedroom and woke me up every two hours so that he could put fresh plasters on. He did this for three nights on the run

– the Wednesday, Thursday and Friday nights before the Arsenal game. He put hot towels on as well, and without him, I'd never have played that day.

'What we used to do was that in the morning, I'd run him to his home in Wallasey before we went over to Goodison for more treatment. I didn't know how he'd stuck it for three nights on end and without much sleep, but he told me he used to try and get a few hours each afternoon before he came back with me to my home in Birkenhead to start putting on the plasters all over again.'

Dean himself had the patience and the desire to do whatever it took to be fit, but it was Harry Cooke's dedication, skill and perseverance that ultimately did the job – as Dixie was cleared for the last game of the season.

As things transpired, Everton were already champions before the Arsenal game was played. Huddersfield Town's title challenge had foundered and then collapsed in the last week of the season. A shock 1-0 home defeat to Sheffield United the previous Saturday was followed by a 3-0 reverse at the hands of Aston Villa, their last remaining game in hand, on the Wednesday. That knowledge took the pressure off the Toffees going into the Arsenal game. Now, they could focus on helping Dean chase down Camsell's record.

Dixie had put a phenomenal 14 goals on Ted Harper's standing Division One record before a ball was even kicked on the last day of the season – so he had already made history. Indeed, that 57-goal tally would still be the top-flight record today had Dixie been unable to add to it. But there was a chance to push what had already been an extraordinary season into the realm of the legendary. And everyone at Goodison Park was determined to help their adored centre-forward do just that.

Liverpool was the focus of the football world on that fateful Saturday. 'Soccer fans from the Merseyside area converged in their thousands on Goodison Park,' wrote Nick Walsh. 'Ferryboats and trains from across the Mersey plus special football trams in Liverpool steamed, purred, and clanged along to convey fans from far and near. The crowds were imbued with the mystic expectancy of a religious pilgrimage, set on bearing witness to some supernatural vision and bathe in its glory. There was no guarantee the spirit would appear, but the slimmest hope was sufficient attraction. Not to be there if it should happen would condemn devout football souls forever to purgatory, a penance Everton fans were determined not to suffer.'

And so the scene was set. 5 May 1928. Everton versus Arsenal in front of a heaving Goodison Park. The last chapter of a scarcely believable story. And what a chapter it proved to be.

Anyone who might have thought that the Gunners would show up on Merseyside and be content to simply make up the numbers or provide Dean with a guard of honour was quickly disabused of such notions. The Londoners were quickest out of the blocks against their somewhat distracted hosts and took an early lead, quelling the roars of the surprised Everton fans. But not for long, as their goalscoring talisman soon drew his side level, powering in a header from a corner. Goal number 58 for Dean.

The game settled and fell into something of a lull, but only for a short period, before all hell broke loose. Dean, taking matters into his own hands, burst into the visitors' box only to be upended. The *Liverpool Echo* reporter felt it was an 'accidental collision', but the referee and the home crowd had no doubts. Penalty kick. 'Give it to Dixie!' chanted the crowd. And they did. Dean placed the ball calmly on the spot before slamming home his 59th goal of the season to equal George Camsell's phenomenal record.

To their credit, amidst all the celebrations, Arsenal maintained their focus, and after a period of domination, they levelled the scoring just on half-time.

Nevertheless, as the two sides retired for their half-time cup of tea, there was only one topic of discussion on the terraces – could Dean take the record outright?

The second half was a different affair, with the Gunners tightening up in defence and seemingly determined not to give Dixie an inch. The clock ticked inexorably on; Goodison Park dripped with tension as the Toffees struggled to create a chance for their centre-forward. Then, with just eight minutes left on referee Harper's timepiece, Everton forced a corner. Alec Troup, their diminutive Scottish winger and supplier of so many of Dean's goals, took the set piece. 'And out of a ruck of probably 14 players,' reported the *Liverpool Echo*, 'Dean, with unerring accuracy, nodded the ball to the extreme right-hand side of the goal.' Goal number 60!

'The roar from the crowd must have reached a thousand decibels,' wrote Nick Walsh. 'The co-ordinate of voices was like a thunder-clap heard throughout the length and breadth of Merseyside.'

Dixie, as was his way, bowed his head modestly, as players from both sides ran to congratulate him. When the game resumed after a stoppage of several minutes, the Everton players appeared to play as if in a dream, and few in the crowd seemed to care. So it probably came as no surprise when Arsenal grabbed a very late equaliser – a reward for their professionalism, which had been representative of all those who had tried to stop Dean throughout the season.

Many had tried, as was evident in match report after match report, and many had failed. But their efforts game after game to thwart him added meaning and weight to his superhuman feat.

News spread quickly around the football world of Dean's extraordinary achievement. Lucrative offers came in from near and far – including from the then booming American Soccer League – designed to entice Dixie away from Everton. His unequalled ability and of course his pulling power were not lost on all interested parties, but Dean was not for moving. Everton were his dream club after all.

Curiously, news of the Everton centre-forward's record-breaking strike got a little lost crossing the Irish Sea, where this story is ultimately headed. The *Sunday*

Independent somehow managed to lose that third goal, reporting the following day that Dean 'by getting two of Everton's goals, one of them a penalty, equalled the scoring record for a season held by Camsell'. The mistake was rectified, however, in Monday's edition of the paper's daily sister, the *Irish Independent*. 'Dixie Dean (Everton), whom Dublin enthusiasts had the pleasure of seeing in action recently, broke the goal-getting record of Camsell (Middlesboro') when he registered a "hat trick" against Arsenal and brought his total of goals for the season to 60 – one more than Camsell's.'

* * *

The anatomy of Dean's 60-goal league season is worth summarising. Indeed, those with an interest in the history of the game should ruminate on his outrageous total.

Dean scored in 29 of the 39 league games in which he played. Of the 60 goals he scored, 40 were scored with his feet and 20 with his head – a testament to the excellence of his all-round game. In the 29 games in which he scored, Dixie bagged eight singles, 14 braces, five hat-tricks, as well as four goals against Burnley at Turf Moor and five against Manchester United at Goodison.

Had he not missed three games for the Toffees due to international and league call-ups, it's entirely likely he'd have pushed his record even higher. Indeed, given he scored at a rate of 1.5 a game in the 1927/28 season, it's not unfair to suggest he might have found the back of the net on at least another three or four occasions.

Dean went on to create yet more records in his wonderful career, but it's the 60-goal season that sets him apart from all who came before and after and that made him one of the first international superstars of the beautiful game's history.

5

Dixie Dean Arrives in Sligo

IN THE shadow of Benbulben mountain lies the town of Sligo, the town's train station and a gathering crowd. It's the morning of Friday, 27 January 1939. Reports say there may have been as many as 2,000 people there to greet the greatest superstar ever to visit the town. It's incredible really. In the 1930s, to consume soccer, you played it, went to watch it or you read about it. Yes, perhaps you might have seen snippets of matches in the cinema on *Pathé News*, but that's all they were, snippets. So for a man who many had probably at best just read about to draw such a crowd on a bleak January, west-of-Ireland morning speaks to the status of William Ralph Dixie Dean.

So the people came in their droves. The club's hierarchy came. *The Sligo Champion* came. Mayor Conlon, a member of the Sligo Rovers committee, came – and they waited. Doubtless many present were there because they didn't really believe. Probably came to snigger and giggle at the most outlandish news the town had ever heard. Others came because they wanted to believe, wanted to see their town on the map, wanted the excitement, the madness.

And the train duly arrives, steaming slowly into the station as if deliberately building the excitement and the tension. And there is a swell of excitement as the passengers alight. Eyes strain, necks crane. The welcome is ready.

But Dixie Dean does not come. William Ralph Dixie Dean is not on the morning train from Dublin. And one can only imagine the disappointment, the shock, as the train empties and the platform clears and the biggest star ever to come to Sligo doesn't in fact come to Sligo.

Imagine how the club officials must have felt? Hearts in mouths. Had it been a ruse? Had they been set up? Were they going to look like fools?

And the fans and the people? Ah, sure it never could happen. What on earth would football's greatest centre-forward be doing coming here? Had everyone lost their heads? Perhaps the report in the *Irish Independent* the previous Tuesday, stating that Dean had only agreed to help find players for the club and that he had 'definitely declined to make a personal appearance', was true after all?

But then a phone call from Dublin, an update and an apology. And relief all round. Dixie Dean said he was coming, and Dixie Dean is coming – but on the later train. He'll be there at 6.40pm. Sincere apologies for the misunderstanding. The former Everton man had taken the opportunity while in Dublin to visit an old friend

– Dean was renowned for his loyalty to friends – the former coach of Bohemians FC and former Evertonian, Billy Lacey.

Volt in *The Sligo Champion* reported on the player's eventual arrival in his 'Soccer Causerie' column the following Saturday.

'While hundreds cheered a welcome to "Dixie" Dean at Sligo station last Friday night, the famous centre-forward tired, yet smiling and happy, told me that the ovation he was receiving was just like an English cup final. Immediately he stepped off the train, he was surrounded by vociferous men, women and children. Following his failure to arrive on the early morning train, there was keen disappointment felt in the town which was quickly banished when the evening train steamed into the accompaniment of exploding fog signals. Rarely, if ever before, did Sligo accord such a royal welcome to anybody. With difficulty, the hero of the hour was brought to the Railway Hotel where he was introduced to members of the Rovers Management Committee.'

The *Irish Independent* reported on Dean's arrival in similarly excited fashion.

'Scenes of extraordinary enthusiasm were witnessed at Sligo G.S.R. [Great Southern Railway] Station on the arrival from Dublin yesterday afternoon of the 6.40 train, which brought to the Sligo Rovers' team the former English international centre-forward, Dixie Dean.

'Over 2,000 people, representative of all classes in the town, thronged the platform. As the train steamed in, fog signals were exploded on the line, and the crowd cheered vociferously.

'Dean was with difficulty escorted to the Great Southern Hotel, which adjoins the railway premises, and later went to the Café Cairo,[5] Wine St., outside of whose doors a dense mass of townspeople continued to wait for several hours for a glimpse of the famous footballer.'

In Dean's own account, the fog signals in his honour certainly left an impression – betraying perhaps a slight trepidation at being an English man in a country that had fought so long and so hard to escape the rule of London. 'They told me there was a big reception waiting for me there and when the train was a mile from Sligo, I heard five explosions. I looked across at the Sligo official and said, "These IRA blokes aren't very good shots are they. They've missed five times!"'

A nervous joke perhaps, but Dean needn't have worried. There's just something about football after all that can transcend almost any barrier. Seems like there always has been. The Sligo welcome he received was as excited and generous as you could expect or imagine.

And as if there wasn't excitement enough, it turned out that Sligo's new striker wasn't the only celebrity in the Great Southern Hotel that evening. Also present was the famous Irish American tenor, Jack Feeney. A native of Swinford in neighbouring County Mayo, Feeney had achieved huge success in the United States and was back

---

5   According to the Sligo Rovers Heritage Group, Dean lodged in rooms above the Café Cairo on Wine Street in the centre of Sligo town during his time with the club.

in Ireland on a short tour. *The Sligo Champion*'s football correspondent, Volt, captured the unlikely meeting of the two stars of very different fields. 'There was an interesting interlude in the hotel when celebrity met celebrity. Dean, surrounded by Committee members and Press representatives, was saying how glad he was to come to Ireland to play and that he would do his very best for the Sligo team when Mr Jack Feeney, famous Irish American tenor walked into the room. The two celebrities were introduced, shook hands and wished each other the best of luck. It was all very interesting but although both men are well known in their own particular lines, I am quite sure that Mr Feeney had never heard of Mr Dean before, or Mr Dean had never heard of Mr Feeney. However, they know each other now.'

It had been quite a day in Sligo, a day for the annals of the town. But this was only the beginning, the prelude. For there was much more excitement to come. Much, much more – beginning with Dixie's debut two days later against Dublin side Shelbourne.

Sligo, Sligo Rovers and Irish football were agog. All eyes were focused on the town. For scarcely in the game's history, anytime, anywhere, can there ever have been a more unlikely signing.

6

Debut – Questions to be Answered

FOR SLIGO Rovers, spectacular coup though it was, the signing of Dixie Dean was nevertheless a gamble. Obviously, his recent injury-dogged seasons were a worry. Football fairy tales aside, the financial element of the story couldn't be ignored. Dean wasn't coming for free, and the club's committee needed him to do more than fill a train station (even if he did do it twice in one day!).

The club had pushed the boat out on this one. The opportunity could hardly have been passed up once it became clear that the player was interested in the move, but help was needed to fund the deal. According to Volt in *The Sligo Champion*, 'were it not for the whole-hearted support of a number of citizens of the town who offered to become guarantors of "Dixie's" wages, the capture would not have been possible. Sligo's finances could not bear the expense.'

With the help of the generous, local benefactors, the club was hopeful that Dean's standing in the game would provide enough pulling power to cover any outlays and earn the club some money on top. A good second half of the season in both league and cup would provide enough fixtures to capitalise on Dean's presence in the side – both in Sligo and wherever else he lined out in their colours.

The league was a long shot. But even if catching a smart Shamrock Rovers side was unlikely, the runners-up spot was worth pursuing. After all, it would have represented the club's second-best league return in its short senior history. And a good run of league form would certainly help generate interest and lucrative attendances.

And with the FAI Cup set to kick off in February, a trophy the club had yet to win, an exciting cup run wouldn't do the coffers any harm at all – especially if the Bit O' Red could make it to the semi-final and final, which historically had drawn large attendances and very decent returns.

Ultimately, the more games Dean played, the more the turnstiles would click – home and away.

Sunday, 29 January 1939, and the league clash with Shelbourne would be the first test of Dean's pulling power and a first chance to assess just what he had left in the tank.

What would happen if he was but a pale shadow of the legend? What if the injuries really had seriously reduced his mobility? What if the ease with which Notts County let him go truly was a red flag Sligo Rovers shouldn't have ignored? What if the decision to retire only months earlier had actually been the correct one after a long and arduous career?

For all involved with the club, the excitement of signing Dean must have been laced with such fears. Sunday and Shelbourne would tell much. Dean had backed himself to do a job for the club, and Rovers were committed now, one way or the other.

Interest was high and a large crowd was expected at the Showgrounds for the 3.15pm kick-off against the visiting Dubliners. But if Sligo's star signing's legs were gone and his ability to play football had gone with them, then just how long would such interest be maintained?

* * *

For Dixie's debut, however, his attendance alone was always going to be enough to draw a large crowd. After all, international celebrities weren't exactly a common phenomenon in the town and surrounding areas, despite the chance meeting of Dean and the great tenor on the previous Friday evening, which was, in truth, a highly unusual alignment of stars.

But even if Dean were to simply walk out onto the Showgrounds pitch and amble around for the afternoon, that might well have been enough for some – to say they saw him on a football pitch in Sligo's red. Happily for the club and its fans, however, and despite showing an understandable level of rustiness, Dixie gave those who had paid good money to see him a taste of what he was all about as a player and the promise of more.

'The road to the ground was jammed with a crowd and cars,' reported the following day's *Irish Press*, 'with number plates indicating trips having been made from the remotest parts of the county.' And on top of those who had made their own way to the ground, many spectators were bussed in from as far west as Westport in County Mayo and as far north as Derry, as the curious and the star-struck joined the club's regular and irregular supporters to witness Dean's debut. Indeed, a record league crowd for the Bit O' Red was packed into Sligo's humble ground, with gate receipts of £157 (€12,000), as reported by the local paper, to see the fabled striker make his first appearance for the Bit O' Red. Cue much rubbing of hands from the Sligo committee. So far so good. They had got the desired effect off the pitch, but how would Dean perform on the field of play?

According to *The Sligo Champion*'s match report, the Dean effect was somewhat mixed. Ironically, it appeared that the presence of Sligo's new signing served to inspire the visiting Shelbourne side while at the same time appearing to distract and inhibit his colleagues, some of whom appeared to suffer a little from stage fright. The result was a ragged Sligo display at odds with the slick and controlled football they had rolled out for much of the season up to that point.

When Dean did get on the ball, his class was more than apparent but at times seemed to trouble his own overawed team-mates more than their opponents. As the reporter from the *Irish Press* put it, 'the Sligo forwards were, if anything, more bewildered than the Shelbourne lads as to what the ex-Everton man was going to do next. Most certainly Dean distinguished himself. He set a new standard in centre-forward play, but I believe he made sacrifices by trying to aid his colleagues instead of simply helping himself to the full. There were many times when he "sold the dummy" to the Shelbourne defenders, but the Sligo forwards couldn't fit themselves into the scheme of things.'

Even without their star signing, Sligo Rovers would have been favoured to win this game on form, and their supporters could have been forgiven for expecting victory to be a foregone conclusion with the former Everton man now leading the line. But Shelbourne, from Dublin's Ringsend, put up a dogged fight and deservedly took the lead on the half-hour. 'Cue silence from the home crowd,' wrote Volt of the *Champion*. 'This wasn't in the script.'

Nevertheless, Dean had started promisingly for his new club, despite finding himself often trailed by as many as three visiting defenders, led by their captain, Bill Little, as they tried to hustle him out of the game. The *Champion*'s correspondent was also clearly preoccupied with Sligo's legendary centre-forward and was unsurprisingly fulsome in his praise. Dean's 'masterly foot control and head work was superb,' he wrote, and 'at times he showed the flashes of genius that made him the top-notcher of centre-forwards.'

And to the delight of the fans and the club's hierarchy, it was Dean, with his team-mates struggling to find a rhythm and looking a little lost, who was to lead the fightback. Although many of his team-mates appeared to be struggling to get on to his wavelength, the former Everton man had been linking well with Sligo's Irish international winger Paddy Monaghan,[6] and the two had been at the heart of the home side's most promising first-half efforts. The *Evening Herald*'s reporter, who was unnamed in the paper's report the next day, made note of how Sligo's outside-left had managed to rise above the fray and play his usual game: 'Dean seemed to be a magnet for the westerners' players, as well as the spectators, but only Monaghan appeared to completely detach himself and get on with his own work.'

And it was the almost instant understanding between the two that saw Rovers get back on terms just on half-time before taking the lead early in the second period. First, Monaghan set up the debutant for the equaliser. 'Just on half-time, Dean struck after a defensive error from the visiting [Liam 'Sacky'] Glen. Thinking he had averted the danger of a Sligo attack by clearing for a throw, he turned his back on the play. Monaghan took full advantage, retrieving the ball before it crossed the touchline, he crossed from the left-hand corner flag where Dean controlled before steering the ball past the Shelbourne keeper [John] Webster.'

Dean then returned the compliment with the second half only a few minutes old. 'Monaghan converged on a perfect long pass from Dean,' reported the *Evening Herald*, to finish impressively and put the home side in front. Sligo were to add another before holding off a storming Shelbourne comeback and hung on somewhat fortunately for a 3-2 victory on a pitch

---

6   Paddy 'Monty' Monaghan is the only player in the club's history to have been capped by Ireland while playing for the Bit O' Red.

that had deteriorated dreadfully over the 90 minutes. 'The ground was in a shocking state. There was mud everywhere from post to post,' reported Socaro from the *Irish Press*, before crediting both sides for dishing up such exciting fare. 'Just how those 22 players kept going as they did beats me.'

None of that mattered, of course, to the Sligo fans and the club committee who left the ground in ebullient form. A record crowd, two points in the bag and, most importantly, hard evidence that Dixie Dean wasn't just a living legend, he was a functioning one to boot.

After the game, Socaro caught up with Dean by phone to get his thoughts on his debut, providing evidence that post-match interviews are clearly not a modern phenomenon! The resulting piece was suitably diplomatic from the Englishman – boosting the league, his club, the Sligo support and outside-left Monaghan, all in very generous fashion.

Dean professed to have been highly delighted with the great reception accorded to him in Sligo. 'They are wonderful people,' he said. Asked about the standard of football based on his initial experiences, Dean described it as 'quite good, but somewhat on the slow side'. But Rovers' new centre-forward was quick to praise the performance of 'Monty' Monaghan – whom he regarded as a 'fine player, who could be developed'. Dean was also impressed with the efforts of Sligo's half-back line.

On playing on a pitch scarcely conducive to quality football, Dean felt that Sligo would be seen 'at their best on more level pitches'. All the boxes were expertly ticked in the interview – with Dean proving himself the consummate professional!

But Dixie and his new colleagues had no time to rest on their laurels. Next up was a trip to Dublin three days later to Shelbourne's home ground of Shelbourne Park – but not to play Sunday's visitors. In fact, Rovers would be lining out against County Wicklow's Bray Unknowns in what was a rather hastily rearranged fixture – and one that must've had all of those involved in the Wicklow club rubbing their hands. For even before Dean had kicked a ball for his new club, Rovers and Bray had agreed to move the rescheduled game from the Wicklow outfit's Carlisle Grounds home to the bigger Dublin venue in anticipation of another bumper crowd. And they were not to be disappointed.

7

Two in Two, but Ringsend Defeat to the Unknowns

FOR THE first 50-odd years of the League of Ireland, the away side picked up around 20 per cent of gross gate receipts for league fixtures. This method of dividing the takings at the gate lasted up until the 1970s. It was designed to help cover the expenses of the travelling team and was most crucial to the clubs outside of Dublin – like Sligo Rovers, Dundalk, Limerick, Cork City and Waterford – as they had many more miles to cover in a season.

However, when the gates collapsed in the capital in the 1970s, there was a move to a flat fee agreement wherein the travelling side received £150 (€1,400). But as times got harder and support for the local game drifted away, even that amount was eventually dropped as fans, money and then generosity became simply too scarce.

Interestingly though, when clubs looked across the Irish Sea for players who might boost attendances during the gloom of the 1970s and 1980s, the likes of Terry McDermott, Trevor Brooking, Jimmy Johnstone, Peter Lorimer and even George Best – all very much at the tail end of their careers – agreements were often reached that saw the sides boasting such crowd-pullers pick up some of any increased gate that resulted from their appearance.

And to complicate matters, such high-profile players were also often offered or insisted upon a percentage of the receipts as part of their contracts. In some ways, the lot of the professional footballer, no matter how successful, hadn't improved that much over the 1930s by this period. When their careers at the top ended, players still couldn't hope of retiring to the golf course or even to the gantry or the television studio, although opportunities within the game as coaches and managers were beginning to expand. Nevertheless, many still had to eke out a living wherever they could. And if that meant playing a few games at lower levels or in Ireland, then so be it. For many, football was all they knew and the only skill they had for trade.

A case in point was World Cup and Manchester United legend Bobby Charlton, who played four times for Waterford United in the 1975/76 season. When Charlton joined the Blues in January 1976, the away side fee had already been ditched several years previously. But club chairman Joseph Delaney revealed that the length of Charlton's contract and hence his stay in Ireland would depend almost entirely on the click of the turnstiles at their Kilcohan Park home and crucially on whether opposing clubs would pay a percentage of their gate receipts when Waterford and Charlton came to play. Moreover, as it later transpired, the player's own contract stipulated a percentage of all gate receipts – a deal that was to unravel within a month.

Healthy crowds did attend his home debut against St Patrick's Athletic on 18 January and at an away fixture in Donegal against Finn Harps the following week. But the tenuous nature of the agreement between club and player was exposed in the next game at Dalymount Park against Bohemians. With some doubt raised over Charlton's cut of the game's receipts, he only announced the day before the fixture that he would be lining out for the visitors. However, the uncertainty around his participation and the late nature of his confirmation seriously impacted the size of the attendance. This, in turn, led Bohemians to refuse to yield any of what turned out be a very disappointing set of gate receipts to the Waterford side.

In fairness to Charlton, reports from the time suggest he had performed honestly on the pitch for his Irish hosts. However, at the grand old age of 39, he clearly no longer had the legs to wow the crowds and pull in the punters. With home gates at Kilcohan Park failing to meet expectations and away sides refusing to share the proceeds earned, it quickly became clear that the deal was unsustainable. Unfortunately and unsurprisingly, Charlton's short stint in Ireland came to a swift and ignominious end in late February as Waterford fell to a sorry 3-0 FAI Cup defeat at the hands of Finn Harps.

Although there are parallels between the Bobby Charlton story and that of Dixie Dean and Sligo, the circumstances were quite different. Perhaps most pertinent was the fact that 1930s football in Ireland was a deal healthier than its 1970s counterpart. When Dean joined Sligo, domestic soccer was drawing decent crowds league-wide, but especially in Dublin and Cork. It was faring well against rival team sports like GAA and rugby and was a long way from the collapse of interest in the domestic product that came in the 1970s, the result of the creeping *Match of the Day* influence on the Irish football public.

* * *

Three days after Dean's encouraging debut, Sligo Rovers made the trip to Dublin to face the mysteriously named Bray Unknowns – perhaps the most self-deprecating club name in the game's history – at Shelbourne's home in Ringsend. The inclusion of their star signing in the travelling party was already set to increase the expected attendance – but the news that Dixie appeared to be in fine fettle only served to swell the numbers.

The switch from Bray's Carlisle Grounds down in Wicklow to the larger Dublin venue made sense for all concerned. Obviously, the 'home' side was set to reap an unexpected reward. The original fixture, pre-Dean, would hardly have seen even their own humble Bray ground packed to the rafters. Hastily rearranging the game in light of the English marksman's arrival on the Irish scene was a fine example of opportunism by the seaside strugglers.

For Sligo Rovers, a big away gate would see their own coffers swell, what with 'Billy Box Office' leading the line. That a crowd of around 4,000 turned up on a chilly Wednesday afternoon in the capital, bringing with it record gate receipts of £192 (€13,500), underlined the enduring pulling power of the player. And the monies taken through the turnstiles were a very welcome February boost for both sides.

However, for the second game in succession, the Bit O' Red struggled to find their form. Their pleasing attacking approach was once again absent, as they struggled to get out of first gear against a game but limited Bray Unknowns side. Indeed, just as Shelbourne the previous Sunday seemed inspired by the thought of facing Dean, so too the Wicklow team appeared to play above themselves. Up to their meeting with Rovers, the Unknowns had amassed a measly five points from their 11 league outings, losing eight times. But inspiration and perspiration saw them run out surprising 3-1 winners on this occasion.

Dean again could hardly have been faulted. Indeed, he showed all his old battling characteristics, suffering a nasty head wound halfway through the first half and ultimately leaving the field of play for prolonged treatment just before half-time. By then, his side were a goal down and his exit was a clear disappointment to the assembled crowd. But all and sundry were delighted when Dean emerged for the second half, his head swathed in bandages.

Unfortunately, his team-mates were unable to match his resolve or powers of recovery. Failing to rouse themselves from their first-half torpor, they continued to be outwitted and outrun by the determined Bray players and unsurprisingly found themselves two down within minutes of the restart.

Dean, despite his head injury, continued to fight and bagged his second goal in two games from a Monaghan corner.

But try as Sligo Rovers might with a brisk wind behind them, they just couldn't force a leveller and were caught four minutes from time as Bray Unknowns nicked a third.

The *Cork Examiner*'s report on the game seems a fair appraisal of the events of that Wednesday afternoon. '**£200 For A Mid-Week Match**' screamed the headline – '**But Sligo Fail – Bray Spoil Westerners' League Chance**.'

Dean was always going to be the story, but as the paper noted, Sligo's defeat more or less meant Shamrock Rovers were now nailed on to retain their League of Ireland crown.

'The drawing powers of Dixie Dean were pleasantly in evidence at Shelbourne Park yesterday, for his appearance proved the lure for so big a crowd that the "gate" reached almost £200, an unprecedented amount for a midweek match of its kind.

'Dean gave a good display and had the honour of scoring one of the goals. It is obvious, however, that this very good player will not be seen at his best until he has become merged, so to speak, in the tactics and general methods of his own forward line. His play was stamped certainly by individuality, and on occasions he gave the big crowd those adroit touches which only the master can command.

'It would be idle to say, however, that there was anything really outstanding in his play. He had the misfortune to be off for 15 minutes with a head injury, and this naturally slowed him up unto very cautious methods.

'This result leaves Shamrock Rovers a 100 per cent certainty to win the league, as Sligo had the best chance of overtaking them if the Milltown team slipped.'

The *Irish Independent* and some of the Dublin crowd were a little more critical of Dean's efforts, however. 'We must pass Dean with the Scottish verdict of "not proven" for he was off the field for fifteen minutes with a head injury sustained in a collision with a couple of Bray defenders. Up to the time of his injury, however, his performance had not been an inspiring one, and Dalton, the Bray centre-half, literally had him in his pocket. Some spectators indulged in ribald comment on Dean's display as a result. When Dean returned after being injured, he showed some nice touches, but never tried to force a passage through the strong Bray defence.'

Perhaps the views were a little harsh. After all, Dean was still finding his feet after a long period out of the game and was still searching for the sharpness and understanding of his new colleagues that would only come with games.

Regardless, the Bray defeat marked another disappointing result and performance from the westerners. But despite Dean's struggles, there was at least some encouragement for Sligo fans in the fact that he still retained the happy knack of finding the back of the net. But more important than that perhaps, he clearly had the determination and the grit of old. Dixie hadn't come to Ireland to simply let his reputation do the work. That, if little else, augured well for the Bit O' Red on the long trip home from the capital.

However, things would get worse for Sligo Rovers before they got better, as they slipped to another defeat the following Sunday in Limerick. Again, the fixture drew a sizable crowd eager to see Sligo's superstar. Unfortunately, however, the former England man didn't figure – Wednesday's head injury was enough for the club's committee to decide to give their prize possession a rest and some recovery time after a whirlwind start.

But if the Limerick crowd were disappointed to miss out on seeing the great man play, at least they saw their side win comfortably 3-0 as Sligo's dip continued and any hope of catching Shamrock Rovers faded from view.

8

FAI Cup Round One – Class is Permanent

WITH A league title out of the question after their recent poor run of form, Sligo Rovers travelled south to Cork for the first round of the FAI Cup a week later. It was their third road trip in two and a half weeks, covering all points east, west and south that the senior domestic game in Ireland had to offer. Given what would have been an expensive run of games for any Irish club, the Sligo hierarchy will at least have been buoyed by the impact on attendances that Dean was having. And they would end up more than pleased on that showery, cold February Sunday, as yet another record crowd turned out at Cork City's Mardyke home to see Dixie play.

As ever, the exact crowd was difficult to pin down – but according to reports, the attendance was somewhere between 11,000 and 20,000 spectators – with *The Sligo Champion* and the *Belfast Telegraph* plumping for the former, while the *Birmingham Mail* went for the higher figure (proving that out of sight wasn't out of mind when it came to Dixie Dean and the English public). Whatever the number, the gate receipts were a handsome £455 (€33,000), half of which Sligo would take home, once the game's expenses had been cleared.

The FAI Cup was Rovers' only hope now of securing silverware, and a good run and good crowds would go a long way to justifying the investment in their English star.

But while the newspapers might not have agreed on the attendance, the performance of Sligo's centre-forward drew gushing praise from all as the westerners ran out 2-1 winners in what was a classic, breathless cup tie.

'Dixie Dean had a lot to say in Sligo Rovers' 2-1 victory over Cork, at Cork, in the Eire Cup. His presence was the means of attracting 11,000 spectators. Dixie played a great game throughout, although he did not score,' reported the *Belfast Telegraph*. (Interestingly, the *Telegraph* also mentioned that there was a rumour that Dean would be returning to Nottingham after the game, hinting that his time with Sligo was already at an end. However, while the player was indeed returning home, it was just to see his family. Rumours and newspapers – the football media really hasn't changed too much over the years!)

Meanwhile, the *Birmingham Mail* was more ebullient in its short report. 'Sligo Rovers, with their attack led by Dixie Dean, beat Cork City by two goals to one in the first round of the Eire Challenge Cup at the Mardyke, Cork, yesterday. A record crowd of 20,000 watched the game, and Dean was mainly responsible for swelling the attendance. He was accorded a wonderful reception and signed hundreds of autographs before and after the match. Dean led the Sligo forwards in brilliant fashion, and engineered the movement which resulted in Monaghan scoring the winning goal. Sligo went ahead with a penalty through [William] Hay, and [Tommy] Davis, ex-Oldham Athletic, equalised early in the second half. Dean was seen to great advantage during the second period, and before making the goal for Monaghan, he struck the woodwork twice. At the conclusion of the game, he was carried shoulder high to the pavilion.'

The *Irish Independent*'s 'special correspondent' was succinct in his praise of Dean, writing simply 'He was brilliant.' Meanwhile, the *Irish Press* were left in little doubt that with Dixie Dean, as with all great players, form is temporary, but class is permanent.

'A fortnight ago Dixie Dean came to Sligo Rovers and since then soccer enthusiasts in the West were wondering if he would fulfil expectations. They know now, and Cork fans know to their cost as it was through his ingenuity that Cork were knocked out.'

However, it's the more considered piece printed in *The Sligo Champion* the following Saturday that's of most interest, giving us as it does a fine insight into the all-round quality of Dean's display on the day.

It's easy to think of him as just a goalscoring machine. The reports from the Shelbourne and Bray games illustrated that he still maintained that deadeye for goal, even if, as yet, the prolific nature of his prior record was yet to be displayed. And those watching and those who had invested had already learned that he was as physically committed to the game and to his employers as ever. But the Mardyke match turned out to be an exhibition of the fuller range of his abilities as a footballer, as Dean led his team, oozing class, guile and skill. And crucially this time, his team-mates appeared to be less awestruck, responding more positively to his presence.

Volt in the *Champion* was blown away, and not just by the stiff Cork breeze. 'Over four hundred Sligo Rovers supporters spent fourteen hours on an excursion train last Sunday, in order to see Cork beaten in the first round of the Challenge Cup of Eire. The thrilling game which they witnessed at the Mardyke made the long journey worthwhile. I have yet to see Sligo play better than they did in this gasp-a-minute game which they won on merit but which might easily have been a draw. There can be no doubt that "Dixie" Dean was Rovers' matchwinner. Without him, I think, Sligo's Cup hopes would have been shattered. The mark of "class" was branded on everything he did, every flick of his head, every body swerve and pass paved the way for a Sligo attack and fast heart beats for City's supporters.'

The match was a ding-dong affair and had the home side provided better support for their Irish international forward Tommy Davis, who was outstanding on the day, Cork might have taken something from the tie.

Dean was shadowed by the 18-year-old Johnny McGowan, who would be capped for Ireland later in his career, and it was the battle between the two that caught the Sligo reporter's eye. The youngster had a fine game; his impressive display helped to keep Dean off the scoresheet. That said, Dean did hit the woodwork twice and gave his young marker and all watching an education on how to exert telling influence on a game whilst being under very keen surveillance.

His movement off the ball and his tactical understanding of the game saw him regularly drop deep, with his shadow in close attendance, creating space time and again for his Sligo colleagues to exploit. It was a lesson to all and sundry. 'Clever as Cork's halves were, they failed in seeing through Dean's idea of deserting leadership and wandering around the half-way line. McGowan dutifully followed, leaving a gap in the centre in which [Hugh] O'Connor and [William] Johnston had many clear runs.'

The deep-lying position Dixie adopted in the Mardyke game was a trademark feature of his play, developed over his career as a response to the increasingly close attention he received from defenders as the opposition sought to counter his lethal goal threat.

Right up to the 1950s, the 2-3-5 or W-M formation was de rigueur across the football world, with the centre-forward always at the point of attack. The great Hungarian side of the 1950s is often considered to have broken that mould, most famously in their 6-3 Wembley win over England in 1953. The game is largely remembered for the confusion and ultimate embarrassment the home side suffered as a result of the deep position taken up by the Hungarian number nine, Nándor Hidegkuti, as directed by their tactical genius of a coach, Gusztáv

Sebes. However, similar positional play was noted as far back as the 1927/28 season in which Dean set his record of 60 league goals.

Dixie would often take up such a starting position, befuddling the opposition defenders and breaking their defensive shape. He would regularly drop right back into his own half of the field to direct affairs, before rejoining the Everton attack with devastating effect. It is probably fair to say that the Toffees didn't build a system of play around Dean's innovative thinking; however, there's enough evidence to show that his positional awareness and reading of the game were ahead of their time. And it's also fair to say that the big crowd in Cork in the second round of the FAI Cup that Sunday in 1939 got a real sense of his genius.

Dean was directly involved in both of the Bit O' Red's goals. In the 15th minute, he showed his strength and touch, holding up a ball from wing-half William Hay before slipping namesake William Johnston into the penalty area with a perfectly timed pass. As Cork's defence panicked, the Sligo attacker was upended, and a spot kick was awarded. Hay dispatched the ensuing penalty to put the visitors a goal to the good.

Dean was getting into his stride now and was clearly enjoying himself. A brilliant dummy created an opportunity spurned by left-half James Graham. Minutes later, he drew seemingly every Cork defender to him before a brilliant through ball sent Monaghan, with whom his relationship on the field of play continued to blossom, clear. But again, the opportunity to put Sligo into a more comfortable lead was spurned.

Buoyed by the fact that they were still in the game despite the slickness of the Sligo display, Cork City fought back to dominate the latter stages of the first half, coming closest when Davis cracked the ball off the crossbar, only for the Rovers defence to scramble the rebound clear. The game was end to end as half-time approached, and it was Dean again who made Sligo's next chance, supplying Monaghan once more, only for the winger to see his effort saved by James Foley in the Leesiders' goal.

And then as if to respond to Davis's earlier, spectacular piledriver, Dixie showed his own shooting prowess. Picking up a short ball from Graham, and with everyone expecting a pass, Dean, with little backlift or warning, unleashed 'a screaming drive that tore for the corner of Cork's net'. But Foley was equal to it and made a terrific one-handed save at the expense of a corner.

At the interval, the crowd was abuzz with talk of the excellence and unpredictability of Dean's display. As Volt put it, 'the crowd began thinking up some new adjective for Rovers' leader, who never does what everybody expects him to do'.

But for all Dean's quality, the home side, roared on by the sizable home contingent, just wouldn't lie down. And four minutes into the second half, they, and striker Davis in particular, got their just reward. A mix-up between the Rovers player-coach Alf Peachey and keeper Dave Cranston saw the Cork forward nip in to hook the ball home. One each, and the home side and their fans had their dander up.

But as they pressed for a lead goal, their good build-up play foundered time and again at crucial moments on the lack of attacking options and support for the hard-running and seemingly irrepressible Davis. Gradually, however, the Bit O' Red recovered their composure, wrested back control and eventually capitalised – with Dean playing a pivotal role in what proved to be the winner.

Dropping deep once more, and again dragging young McGowan far from his defensive home, Dean turned and played Johnston through on the right. He in turn laid it off to the onrushing Monaghan who scored with a fine low drive.

The Leesiders responded gamely, but Sligo Rovers resisted, and the tie ended fittingly, according to Volt, 'with the ball at the feet of man of the match, Dixie Dean.

'Cork fought well to the last minute and the team and supporters were good losers. It was, indeed, one of the cleanest cup games I've ever seen. Play the ball was the motto and there will be few grievances to be nursed as a result.'

Sligo's best performance of the season to date had seen them through to the next round – skipping over the tricky Mardyke hurdle. From the media's point of view, none of those attending could complain about the entertainment. For the Cork fans, there may have been disappointment, but for those amongst them drawn to see a living legend playing in the flesh and doing so with such wit and quality, there would be great memories.

For Sligo Rovers and their supporters, the dream of adding a first FAI Cup to the club's trophy cabinet was very much alive. And with Dixie Dean in their ranks and their side now showing signs of being inspired rather than intimidated by his presence, the four hundred or so fans who made the epic journey to Cork for the match returned home to tell the tale with a strong sense that this could indeed be their year.

9

Bread and Butter
But Another Injury

A WEEK later, it was back to the bread and butter of the league and the visit of Louth side Dundalk to the Showgrounds. The two teams were jostling for the League of Ireland runners-up spot behind a Shamrock Rovers side that was disappearing from view, and another healthy crowd had bustled in to view proceedings.

It was their third meeting of the season, with each previous affair – in the Shield in September and the first round of league games in November – having ended up at one apiece. Indeed, the Lilywhites, as Dundalk were known, were something of a bogey side for Sligo Rovers. The Bit O' Red had only ever beaten them once in senior football.

So if the smart money was on another draw, then the smart money showed great insight. A game of few chances, with a few flashes of good football, ended up one each once more! According to the match report in *The Sligo Champion*, 'Half-backs were supreme and defences too steady, aided by a treacherous ground which became greasy after a heavy shower.'

An own goal after a misjudgement by the home side's keeper, Cranston, gave the visitors an early lead. But Sligo Rovers hit back quickly – and once again, it was Dixie Dean who led the home side's response, 'his cleverness again in evidence in making openings for the inside men' despite the close attentions of Dundalk's veteran English defender Henry Hurst.

Within minutes, Sligo were level – the dynamic duo of Dean and Monaghan once again pulling the strings.

'Monaghan took the ball in his stride down the centre and transferred to Dean. O'Connor, lying unmarked, took the centre-forward's pass and sent a great shot beyond [Charlie] Tizard' in the visitors' goal.

Dean then almost grabbed the lead for his team with a superb effort from distance, only to be thwarted by the spectacular efforts of the Dundalk keeper. And that was about as good as the game got, the second half rather petering out as conditions grew increasingly unfavourable underfoot.

Honours even and the runners-up spot still up for grabs. Next up in the league for Dixie's men, another trip to Dublin – this time to face mid-table Drumcondra.

* * *

Suppose you knew in advance that the star attraction for a football game wasn't going to be fit enough to play. But you also knew that making that public knowledge would put a rather large hole in your attendance figures and hence your gate receipts. What would you do?

Perhaps it's unfair to suggest that anything untoward happened around Drumcondra's Tolka Park ground the following weekend when it became clear that Dixie Dean wouldn't be in the Sligo Rovers 11. But as we know from the player's time back in England, the fact that he would be missing wasn't always relayed to those who were prepared to part with hard-earned money to see him perform.

The bald fact of the matter was that the Drums saw their biggest crowd of the season of in or around 10,000 fans, according to the *Belfast Telegraph*, paying a very tidy £216 (€15,300) to watch the visit of Sligo Rovers and their legendary goalscorer. However, Dean was absent through injury. And although he did walk out onto the Tolka Park turf to acknowledge the assembled crowd, many of those present were unable to contain their displeasure on discovering at that point that this was all they would see of him that day. In fact, this was probably the only time in Dixie Dean's stay in Ireland where the reception of the crowd was less than warm.

WPM of the *Irish Independent* takes up the story. 'The biggest attendance of the season turned up at Tolka Park yesterday to see the far-famed Dixie Dean in action but there was no Dixie Dean playing. The Dublin "fans" were annoyed, and they had every right to be … The Limerick public a couple of weeks ago turned up at the Markets Field to see Dean, and he wasn't on the team. It's the old story of "Wolf, wolf", and I fancy that the next time the public will need a guarantee before they go to see Dixie Dean in action. Dean came out in his ordinary clothes to shake hands with the referee and captains but was received with a storm of boos and hisses.'

Although the *Evening Herald* reported on the Wednesday before the fixture that Rovers had 'intimated' to the Drums that Dean would figure, Sligo's committee claimed after the game that they had informed their hosts on the Saturday that as a result of a ligament injury picked up playing golf, the striker would not be getting togged out the following day.

However, for whatever reason, that message wasn't conveyed to those so looking forward to seeing the great man in action in Dublin. Talking to the press after the game, the Drumcondra club secretary, J.F. Levins, claimed he received a telegram from Sligo Rovers late on the Saturday night on his return home, and a notice was posted outside the ground to the effect that Dean would not be playing.

Be that as it may, the large crowd who turned up the following day clearly didn't get the message. Perhaps there really was no time to get word out that Sligo's star at best would be on waving duty. And to give Drumcondra the benefit of the doubt and take Levins at his word, it would seem that the Dublin side had few options given how late they received the unhappy news. It was the 1930s after all – so the means to spread the word (if indeed they truly wanted to) were limited. That said, both clubs certainly benefited from the fact that those who strolled along the banks of the Tolka River, down

Richmond Road or up from Ballybough to the game that Sunday afternoon did so in the belief that they would be seeing one of the biggest names in world football – indeed, the most famous player ever to figure in the Irish game. Doubtless, however, the bean counters at both clubs probably felt they could live with the crushing disappointment of those in attendance when they divvied up the takings on the Sunday evening.

In the end, the many souls present saw the home side lucky to escape with a point as Sligo Rovers failed to convert their greater quality into goals. 'The game was an example of Rovers' unfortunate streak of bad luck in league matches,' reported Volt of the *Champion*. 'It was one they should have won and in each half their superiority over the Drums was clearly marked … Without Dean there was more bustle than cleverness in Sligo's forwards, but their play did deserve greater reward.'

According to his match report, Drums keeper Hurley had a stunning match, topped off with a penalty save from Gerry McDaid in the second half.

Rovers did take the lead through O'Connor just after half-time, but the home side pegged them back with 13 minutes left to play. Missed chances rued, Volt was left to reflect on the obvious – that had Dixie Dean featured, Sligo's chances of winning the game would have been much improved. Indeed, had he played, and Sligo won, the home crowd may well have gone home happy all the same, having seen the legendary centre-forward in action.

* * *

Dixie's injury meant that a late fitness check the following Saturday would decide whether he would be available for the second round of the FAI Cup the following day. The Bit O' Red had a pretty favourable home draw, welcoming Leinster Senior League side Distillery to the Showgrounds for the tie.

'If Sligo play their usual game and refuse to be upset by Distillery's bustling tactics,' read *The Sligo Champion* preview, 'they should win by a comfortable margin.' This was the view with or without their star player, who was fast becoming Sligo's main creative force. And as events transpired, it was the latter, as Dean's golf knee niggle meant he wouldn't be risked.

Demand for Dixie's services didn't stop in Sligo, however. On the same page as the cup match preview, the *Champion* reported that, 'At the emergency meeting of the Connacht Football Association, held during the week, it was decided to ask Dixie Dean to act as referee for the Sligo–Letterkenny game in Letterkenny on St Patrick's Day (17 March), and we are informed that Dixie has consented.'

The game in question was to involve inter-county selections from Sligo and Donegal in a match arranged by the Connacht FA and Letterkenny Crusaders AFC. Ten Donegal towns were to be represented – the first time in many years that Donegal had fielded an inter-county side. Without a League of Ireland club of their own at the time, many fans from the county often travelled to the Showgrounds to watch the Rovers. The more so in recent fixtures, given the scarcely believable presence of the former Everton star in their side.

Dean's trip to Donegal caused quite a stir, despite the fact that he wouldn't actually be playing. This time, the fans were well aware of the fact, and seemed quite content that he would be just officiating the fixture. Even that was an opportunity not to be missed! Amazingly, special buses were laid on across the county to bring fans to witness him man the whistle. But the fans didn't just gather to see the game, for there was to be an added attraction that evening in the town – Dixie had agreed to give a lecture on football and how the great game should be played that St Patrick's evening!

'At eight o'clock Dixie Dean will give a very interesting lecture in the Wolfe Tone Memorial Hall on Modern Football Tactics,' reported the *Derry Journal* the previous weekend.

'This is an opportunity that has never before been offered the sporting public in Donegal. If there is anything anyone wishes to know about football, or any rules explained, "Dixie" will be delighted to answer all questions put to him.'

And there were plenty of people who did want their football questions answered and many more who wanted to witness his appearance as a referee! Dean packed out the hall in what was a very successful enterprise for the organisers, having drawn a crowd of over 1,000 people to the cricket meadow in Letterkenny for the inter-county affair earlier that day, where he was accorded a rousing reception, according to the Derry paper. Possibly the first and only time a football referee was ever greeted in such a fashion!

For the record, the game itself turned out to be a rather one-sided affair, with the stronger Sligo county selection easily overcoming their Donegal rivals in a 7-2 rout. But the crowd really didn't mind – basking as they did in Dean's mere presence, marvelling at his wonderful whistle work!

* * *

Dixie's successful trip north turned out to be a decent distraction for the striker who by then had been out injured for around a month, last kicking a ball in anger against Dundalk on 19 February. In that period, he missed his side's draw against Drumcondra, their laboured victory over Distillery in the cup and a pulsating 4-3 win over Cork City that gave new impetus to their quest for the league runners-up spot. A dim view of the game of golf, however, must have been taken by the club's committee and its fans over those few weeks.

Leinster Senior League side Distillery, from Distillery Road in Drumcondra, were not expected to prevent Sligo from qualifying for the semi-finals of the FAI Cup. And while that did prove to be the case, the unfancied amateurs, with a mixture of grit and physicality, made the favourites sweat for their 2-1 victory and will have been disappointed not to have taken Sligo back to Dublin for a replay.

On a poor playing surface on a cold March Sunday – 5 March, to be exact – Rovers struggled to find a rhythm without their talisman as the visitors snapped into every tackle. Goals either side of half-time from William

Johnston and Gerry McDaid looked to be enough to see Sligo through, but as the final whistle was blown, they were thankful for keeper Dave Cranston's heroics – his second-half penalty save after the plucky visitors had halved the arrears ultimately broke Distillery hearts.

Not a game for the crowd of just under 3,000 to remember with any great fondness – but at least they now had a cup semi-final to look forward to.

A week later, it was back to the league and the visit of Cork City. Dean's absence saw a drop-off in the Showground attendance, with less than 2,000 paying at the gate. But those who did show up at least got their money's worth, with Sligo edging the Cork men with the odd goal in seven! Nevertheless, the westerners' committee were clearly concerned about Dean's fitness and introduced a couple of additional attacking options in the game.

New signing Edward Seddon, described by *The Sligo Champion* as 'a Dixie Dean protégé', had arrived from England the previous day. A product of Bolton Wanderers' nursery, he slotted in at inside-left for his speedy debut.

And a familiar face at the Showgrounds, striker Denis Thompson, who had left Sligo Rovers at the beginning of the season and had spent several months at Exeter, deputised for the injured Dean. According to Volt, Thompson's surprise return was down 'to the anxiety of the committee to find a reserve centre-forward' before the all-important cup semi-final should Dixie's prolonged spell of injury continue.

Both signings impressed, with the latter bagging two of Sligo's goals and bringing a little succour to the worried Rovers hierarchy and two more points in the race for second place.

But as events would transpire, those worries would be blown away the following Sunday when Sligo welcomed the Blues of Waterford to the west.

10

Five of the Best

DEAN'S LIGAMENT injury had kept him off the field of play, refereeing in Letterkenny aside, since mid-February. So with Sligo Rovers entering the final straight in the league neck and neck with Dundalk in the race for the runners-up spot and with the same outfit now confirmed as their opponents in the FAI Cup semi-final, which was just weeks away, concern was growing that the English hitman would struggle to make his presence felt in either.

Thankfully, however, Dixie was well on the road to recovery, with his comeback game pencilled in for 19 March, two days after his successful day and night out in Donegal. And well may the visiting Waterford side have wished that his knee injury had troubled him for just a day longer, as Dean put on the kind of coruscating display that had helped make him the most feared centre-forward in the game's history.

Indeed, the Bit O' Red turned in one of their most impressive attacking performances of the season. Dean's return obviously gave them a lift. But with the trip to Dalymount Park in Dublin to play Dundalk in the cup semi-final next on the agenda, it was clear that many of those in red and white were playing for their places in what would be their biggest game of the season to that point. If the fixture against the Blues of Waterford was an audition for the home side, then all involved made a strong case for a place in the cup showdown cast.

The visitors were slaughtered, seven goals to one, and Dixie Dean was unstoppable, bagging five of Sligo's tally. 'Rovers' leader made goalscoring look easy, but into every effort, he put a touch of class that soon had Waterford's defence bewildered,' reported Volt in the local paper.

But news of Dean's comeback performance travelled much further afield, with Ranger in the *Liverpool Echo* relaying the story back to Dixie's home town thus: 'Our old friend Dixie Dean has been on the warpath again. He got five goals, including a hat-trick for Sligo Rovers in their recent match, two of them headers, and the rest those old-time unstoppable, make-a-hole-in-the-net shots. Dean has been unlucky with strains and sprains since he crossed the Channel, but at last the Sligo folk are seeing what they had been waiting for, for weeks.'

Oddly, it was Waterford who had started the better on the surprisingly dry and bumpy Showgrounds pitch, playing with a pace and intensity that discomfited Sligo and the healthy home attendance. 'Few amongst the crowd, who paid £90 [€6,400],' wrote Volt, 'foresaw the ensuing rout.'

But despite the quality of Waterford's first-half showing, they couldn't find the back of the home side's net and were made to pay, twice, by the returning hero. Dean's first came on five minutes. Pouncing on a long ball out of defence by Denis Thompson, he lashed the ball past the Waterford keeper 'who was probably the most surprised man in the grounds!'

Dean punished the visitors again 15 minutes later, capitalising on poor marking at a corner to nod home Sligo's second.

Waterford may have felt hard done by when the half-time whistle blew, but their plight was to worsen both quickly and dramatically in the second 45. Within five minutes of the restart, they trailed by three as Dean piled on the agony. Dixie was baring his teeth now, and he had little interest in the feelings of the hapless visitors. 'Hay slammed the ball to [Matthew] Began, a deft turn and pass to Dean followed, and the ball was in the net, carefully guided out of Rohan's reach.'

Waterford belatedly pulled one back on the hour, but on 64 minutes, three became four for Dean and the Bit O' Red as the great centre-forward burst between Waterford's central defenders to plant outside-left Mattie McPeake's precise cross neatly past the dejected Waterford keeper.

The visitors visibly wilted, fatigued no doubt from having played only two days earlier against Drumcondra, and conceded goals in quick succession to Began and Seddon, before Dean crowned his display with his fifth and Sligo's seventh just on full time.

The former Everton man had been unplayable. 'Dean's brilliance made the win possible,' wrote Volt. 'It would be safe to say that if he tried for more goals, he could have brought his total to seven.' The *Cork Evening Echo* concurred and purred about Dixie's performance in the second period against the bewildered Blues: 'In the second half, the former Everton star did much as he wished.'

A month off certainly seemed to have helped Dean, his recuperation assisted, according to the match report in the *Evening Herald*, by a return to Everton's Goodison Park for treatment on his troublesome knee and the opportunity to see his family again. Reinvigorated and repaired, Dean had clearly settled into his surroundings, developed a greater understanding of his team-mates and acclimatised to the often-treacherous pitches of the Irish winter and spring. But perhaps most crucially of all, Dixie had regained his match sharpness, and seemed poised to drive his club forward across the final weeks of the season.

* * *

With Waterford sent packing, all thoughts now turned to Dalymount Park in Dublin's north inner city, the spiritual home of the game in Ireland, venue for the FAI Cup semi-final clash with Dundalk the following weekend.

Dean's return could not have come at a better time. There was little doubt that he would be the first name on the team sheet for the fixture – but who else would be joining him? Volt discussed the matter in *The Sligo Champion* on the eve of the big game – and it was clear that excitement about the trip to Dublin was being accompanied by just as much tension if his piece is anything to go by.

'**Cup Selection Amazes Fans**' blazed the headline in the paper on the morning before the game. And Volt was more than a little forthright when it came to his opinion of the Sligo committee's team for the Dalymount clash, which had been picked the previous Thursday.

'Why the committee have passed over Seddon and McPeake takes some explaining and none is forthcoming,' he chided. Volt had been particularly impressed by both in Rovers' recent games and felt that they had done enough, particularly against Waterford, to command starting positions. 'The selection is definitely a bad one, so bad that supporters have been left in amazement. Cup matches, and especially in the semi-final stage, are certainly not the place to try experiments. The decision to drop Seddon is inexplicable. If a place could not be found on the left flank, he could have supplanted O'Connor who has been off form for his last few matches. And his inclusion would have put a dash into the attack, which it sadly lacks.

'A better selection would have been: Cranston, McDaid, Thompson, Hay, Peachey, Johnston, Began, O'Connor, Dean, Seddon and McPeake. That is the team with one change that made the rout of Waterford last Sunday and on that display, they were good enough to beat Dundalk. The selected combination is weaker and is certain to take Rovers out of the position of favourites.'

The very thought of Dundalk clearly made the Sligo correspondent jumpy – with the westerners never having bested the Louthmen in senior football and having come a cropper against them on three previous occasions in the cup – a 4-0 defeat in 1934 in Oriel Park while Sligo were still in the Leinster Senior League, a crushing semi-final defeat the following season (Sligo's first-ever appearance at that stage of the competition) and another shattering cup knockout two seasons later.

Volt's worried opinion piece ahead of the Dalymount matchup was backed up with an angry letter to the editor from a fan printed on the sports page that showed how the anxiety of *The Sligo Champion*'s soccer correspondent was shared by the Sligo Rovers fans. It read:

> Dear Sir – for seven years Sligo Rovers have played in Cup games. With the exception of one year when they were beaten in the semi-final – by Dundalk – they have gone out in the opening rounds.
>
> This year they have a better chance to win the Cup and the committee have selected a weaker team than is at their disposal. As one consistent Sligo supporter I cannot understand their action in dropping Seddon and McPeake. Is it yet too late to ask the committee to reconsider their decision and field a team that will have some chance of reaching the final?

In making the suggestion that Seddon or McPeake should be put on the team I do so in no spirit of prejudice against any player but because of a long-standing desire to see Rovers win the Cup.

Yours Faithfully – Old Supporter

Cup fever clearly was taking a grip in the town! There was a real sense that with Dean prominent in a developing team, this could be their year. An opportunity not to be missed.

While the league has always presented us with irrefutable evidence as to who is the best team in the land, the challenge cup competition has always been a different animal, built to a very large extent on romance and dreams. Up until relatively recent times in England, this was still very much the case. And for smaller clubs, perhaps that magic still remains. However, the advent of the Premier League and the Champions League, and the astonishing riches even just surviving in the former and qualifying for the latter bestow, has relegated domestic cup competitions to nuisance value for too many clubs.

Back in the 1930s (and the 40s, 50s, 60s, 70s and even the 80s) though, winning the FA Cup was a very big deal indeed. The final itself was the domestic season's showpiece. The semi-finals, however, often eclipsed the Wembley final for drama, being as they were exercises in tension, glory and heartbreak.

In Ireland, the romance of the Irish equivalent endures, however – and whilst it too has suffered over the years with the drop-off in interest in the domestic game, relatively decent crowds still attended cup games and cup finals by and large (the dark days of the late 1970s and 1980s aside), especially when one of the provincial sides was in the running.

And as the gradual rebirth in interest in domestic fare has slowly become apparent, the swelling of the cup-final crowd at Lansdowne Road in recent seasons has been a notable feature. Indeed, the last two finals before the pandemic, in 2018 and 2019, drew crowds in excess of 30,000, while the 2021 edition when pandemic restrictions on attendances had been lifted produced a gate of 37,126 – figures not really seen on a consistent basis since the 1950s. And as if to underline the pulling power of the garrison clubs and the provincial teams, when Sligo Rovers last won the FAI Cup in 2010, 36,000 souls were there to see the penalty shoot-out win over Shamrock Rovers.

There is an enduring magic and excitement in one-off cup ties. A tension that the bread and butter of the league can naturally lack. And that tension and excitement was hitting Sligo hard 80 years ago in late March 1939, as Volt's strident criticism of the committee's team selection and the fan letter to the editor of *The Sligo Champion* make plain.

One can only wonder how the committee's 11 might have gone down today on the likes of Twitter! Talk about a Sligo fuming meltdown!

But as we'll see, that tension and those passions were to be stoked even further in the weeks that followed in quite extraordinary circumstances.

11

Dundalk at Dalymount – Drama On and Off the Pitch

AS THINGS transpired, Volt and the Old Supporter need not have worried, as their side, once again directed by the experience, calmness and quality of Dixie Dean, saw off Dundalk in a dramatic Dalymount encounter. That said, both will have been hanging on to their hats as Sligo scrapped and scraped their way to their first ever FAI Cup Final.

A crowd of 24,412 turned out on Sunday, 26 March at the Phibsborough ground to watch a pulsating game full of incident between the two provincial powerhouses of Irish football.

One fan of the Bit O' Red told *The Sligo Champion* on leaving the ground that the last ten minutes were the most nerve-racking he'd ever witnessed at a football match.

'Sligo one goal up – Dundalk draw level – Began scores the winning goal, twenty-four thousand throats roar or groan,' wrote Volt in a breathless match report, 'and there you have the Sligo–Dundalk game in a nutshell.'

'There were other thrills in this game and other gasps. Dean's mistake [more on that later], Cranston's do-or-die dive and three scramble them in at all costs goals, two of them giving Rovers entry to the final against Shelbourne.

'Both sides showed the strain and nervousness inseparable from Cup games. All the players, with the exception of Dean who was as cool and imperturbable as ever, failed to reach League form. The ball might have been filled with explosives so quickly did they try to get rid of it.'

It was probably of little surprise that many of the players involved might have frozen a little on what was a very big stage for the vast majority of them. Dean certainly wasn't fazed, having been used to playing in front of average crowds of around 30,000 in his Goodison Park days.[7] And while attendances of over 20,000 were not entirely unusual in Ireland for big cup ties, playing in front of such an attendance in a one-off, winner-takes-all affair was bound to turn many a knee to jelly.

Although today, FAI cup semi-finals are treated like any other round of the competition in terms of venues, there was a time when the penultimate ties were always played at neutral grounds. Indeed, on this semi-final weekend, nearly 37,000 spectators paid in to see the games

---

7   Another reason why Dean may have felt more comfortable than many of his colleagues and opponents that day in the febrile surrounds of Dalymount Park was because the ground was designed by Archibald Leitch, Britain's foremost football stadium architect, who had also designed Dixie's beloved Goodison Park.

at Dalymount and the all-Dublin clash of Shelbourne and Bohemians at Shamrock Rovers' Milltown home.

So nerves may have got the better of some at Dalymount – but it's worth considering that both sets of players were running out in front of an attendance that wasn't far off the combined populations of the towns of Sligo and Dundalk at that time!

On the field of play, the County Louth side had the better of the early exchanges and looked the more likely side in the first half. A second FAI Cup Final in two seasons looked very much on the cards for the Lilywhites. But a positional switch in the second half when George Thompson moved to right full-back and Gerry McDaid to left-half helped Sligo Rovers find their fluency, and the Bit O' Red gradually grew into the match, becoming more and more dominant the longer the second half went on.

Despite the excitement it generated, the match reportedly had few clear-cut chances. A tale of two goalkeepers, according to Volt. 'Cranston took risks, some of them justified, some not, but he gave a daring display of goal keeping. [Charlie] Tizard made two mistakes, to which Dean and his full-backs contributed, and they lost Dundalk that long-awaited chance of winning the Cup.'[8] Socaro in the *Irish Press* was of like mind: 'Twice Tizard was at fault and paid dearly for his slight errors of judgement. Cranston paid the penalty once, but got off scot-free on other occasions when his sense of anticipation was at fault.'

---

8   Dundalk had appeared in three previous finals in 1931, 1935 and 1938 – losing on each occasion.

As in the recent league meeting between the sides, Dean was once again subject throughout the game to the close attentions of Dundalk's half-back Henry Hurst and had few opportunities to score. However, Sligo's centre-forward was still at the heart of the westerners' best moments. 'Hurst was impressive in charge of Dean who found he had little scope from the opposition pivot. His efforts were mainly confined to making openings, but of these he made plenty. Three times the inside forwards were slow in anticipating his clever "leaves" which gave a clear path to goal.'

Ultimately, Dean's ability to read the game and make space and chances for his team-mates proved crucial, and despite the 'splendid' efforts of their Irish internationals Mick Hoy, Billy O'Neill and Dicky Lunn, Dundalk's seemingly impenetrable defence 'fell,' wrote Volt, 'to the wiles of Dean.'

'In the 10th minute, Dean taking the ball from the dead ball line turned it into Dundalk's goal. O'Neill and Tizard had it well covered, but O'Connor nipped in to score the opening goal. Seven minutes later, Dundalk equalised. Cranston was at fault in failing to hold Dicky Lunn's free kick. Instead, he half punched, half palmed the ball into a bobbing group of players. Three times Donnelly and McArdle tried to force the ball through and on the fourth rebound McArdle lashed it into the net.'

One each at the interval, but in truth the score may have flattered the Connacht side. However, the positional change mentioned earlier seemed to alter the flow of the game, and for the first 35 minutes of the second half,

Rovers were on top, bagging what turned out to be the winner in the 57th minute.

'Against the breeze in the second half, Sligo were a better team. The winning goal came in the 12th minute of this half. Between the full-backs Dean pivoted once more and as he was the centre of attention he let Began through to score from close range.'

Strangely, on reading the various reports on the semi-final, the match is often remembered for a peculiar incident involving Dean in which he could have put the game to bed. In the 85th minute, he shrugged off Hurst's attentions and had a clear run on Dundalk's goal. However, as he bore down on Tizard in the Lilywhites net, he clearly felt that there had either been an infringement or that he may have been offside, or maybe he thought he heard a whistle, for he looked back over his shoulder as if in a rare display of doubt. Hurst, according to Socaro's account, had called for handball, but it wasn't clear if this was what was on Dean's mind.

But the striker's apparent indecision seemed to have been communicated to Tizard, leaving the keeper seemingly unconcerned, also believing something was awry, as Dixie approached his penalty area having slowed to a trot. To the amazement of all watching, Dixie appeared to pull up a yard or two from the Dundalk keeper and then flick the ball somewhat softly to one side with the goal at his mercy. 'It was not an attempt to score,' wrote Socaro. All this time, Tizard simply looked on feeling no challenge was necessary. As Dean turned away, the Dundalk man then strolled over to pick up the ball. But to the surprise of both players, and the surprise of all present, the referee, a Mr Snape, motioned play on – as he hadn't in fact blown his whistle at all. He too must have wondered what on earth was going on!

The odd incident and their unlikely let-off breathed new life into Dundalk, and they threw everything they had at Sligo in the closing stages of the game.

'If football were governed like petrol engines, I could truthfully say that Dundalk put the accelerator to the floorboard after that escape,' wrote Volt. 'Desperately they stormed Rovers' goal. Corner kick followed corner kick with Cranston having the busiest 10 minutes of his career. Defence was thrown to the winds but the equaliser failed to come. Sligo Rovers were in their first Cup final.'

A massive moment for the club and its players that was celebrated on and off the pitch with equal excitement and exuberance.

* * *

Thoughts, however, turned very quickly to the final where Sligo would meet Dublin side Shelbourne, who had beaten Bohemians 1-0 in the other semi-final the day before. Excitement levels, already high at the thought of the semi-final, were ratcheted up even more with the promise of a day out in the capital and a first FAI Cup Final for the club and its supporters. However, tensions were rising too, as a dispute over just when the final would be played threatened the fixture itself and Rovers' participation therein.

A glum-looking Dean at Notts County in 1938 –
better days in Ireland were just around the corner.

The Giant of Goodison Park – Dean mural towers over houses close to Everton's home

The Showgrounds in Sligo – the heartbeat of the town

Waxwork of Dean bedecked in England livery in Madame Tussaud's of London. The photo, taken in 1929, was a measure of Dixie's fame.

The Dixie Dean Hotel in Liverpool's Football Quarter – just across Victoria Street from The Shankly Hotel

W. R. DEAN

NO. 38 OF A SERIES OF 50

Dixie on a Godfrey Phillips Spot the Winner Cigarette Card from 1937

Statue of Dean at the gates of his beloved Goodison Park

Everton FC – champions of England in Dean's 60-goal season of 1927/28. Dixie is front and centre. Trainer Harry Cooke, who was to play a central role in the season's dramatic climax, is top right.

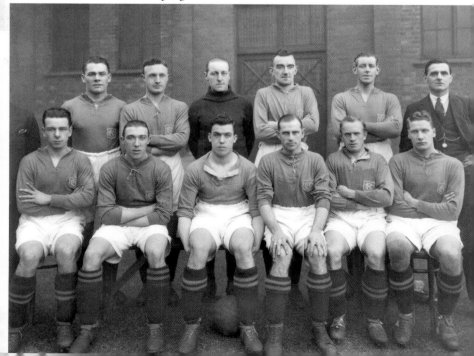

Captain and player-coach Alf Peachey leads Sligo Rovers out for the Dalymount Park denouement. Courtesy of the Sligo Rovers Heritage Group

Captains Little of Shelbourne (left) and Peachey of Sligo (right) join referee Mr Hartles for the cup final coin toss. Courtesy of the Sligo Rovers Heritage Group

Dixie heads home to put the Bit O' Red one up in the decider. Courtesy of the Sligo Rovers Heritage Group

The official programme of the 1939 FAI Cup Final replay. Courtesy of the Sligo Rovers Heritage Group

THE

Football Association of Ireland

Official Programme

(Issued by the Bohemian Football Club Ltd., by authority of the F.A.I.)

CUP FINAL (RE-PLAY)

SHELBOURNE

v.

SLIGO ROVERS

AT DALYMOUNT PARK

Wednesday, 3rd May, 1939

PRICE 2D.

No. 1642

1st Prize £1. 2nd Prize 10/-.
3rd Prize 5/-.

Please keep this Programme, as result of Draw will be announced after half-time.

Jos. I. Wickham
Secretary.

Rapid Printing Co., 60 Middle Abbey Street, Dublin.

A 1939 FAI Cup Final runner-up medal – much like the one returned to Dean at the Dublin Packet almost seven years after the game. Courtesy of the Sligo Rovers Heritage Group

Just a day after their hard-fought victory at Dalymount Park, word filtered through to the club that Shelbourne were looking to have the season's blue-riband clash moved from the appointed date of Sunday, 23 April to the day before – Saturday, 22. From this remove, one could be forgiven for wondering why such a suggestion could result in the ensuing mass protest in the shadow of Benbulben – and the threat not only of the club's withdrawal from the competition, but to its very existence! But the proposed date change had just that effect.

'In the event of this reported application being granted, we request that Sligo Rovers withdraw from the competition and wind up the club in Sligo.'

The above statement was contained in a resolution passed at a meeting of Sligo Rovers supporters held to protest Shelbourne's reported application in Sligo Town Hall on Wednesday, 29 March.

The Sligo Champion reported that the town's mayor, Michael Conlon, who presided over the gathering of some 500 supporters, was keen to point out that 12 months previously, the Football Association's council had decided to play the final on the Sunday and that Shelbourne's representative was present when that date was chosen and offered not a word of opposition. He also warned the game's other provincial clubs – Cork, Dundalk, Waterford and Limerick – that they could face a similar situation in future if the reported application were accepted.

But why such angst and drama? And why the threats not only to withdraw from the final but from senior football altogether? And why should the other clubs mentioned by Conlon have been similarly concerned? Put simply, at the time, the provincial clubs preferred to play their matches on Sundays. Saturdays in the market towns, rural hinterlands and farms outside of Dublin were largely workdays for the supporters of these clubs – so, in this instance, switching the final to the Saturday would deprive a great many Sligo Rovers fans of the chance to attend the game, and it would set a potentially dangerous precedent that could see similar switches imposed on the provincial clubs and their supporters in future. The city clubs tended to favour Saturday fixtures, and if the Football Association were to agree with Shelbourne's request, it would suggest a level of favouritism towards the bigger clubs from the capital, who already possessed many advantages over their outlying rivals. It was the thin edge of the wedge and so the suggestion could not be let stand.

Fairness to the supporters of each club would surely suggest that the day of the final should matter less to the Dublin club – after all, the game would be on their doorstep – a short walk, cycle, bus or tram ride away. However, as things transpired, the Shelbourne concerns revolved less around the fate of their supporters and more around the availability of one of their players, their talismanic international left-winger Tom Priestley who, as a devout Belfast Presbyterian, was not available to play on the Sabbath day.

Or at least that's how things were seen through a Sligo lens. Volt's 'Soccer Causerie' column on Saturday, 1

April made plain the westerners' concerns. 'It is scarcely necessary to give reasons why supporters are perturbed at the suggestion to change the date of the final. There are thousands of them who could not travel on Saturday, and it is apparent that if the official decision is varied an injustice will be done to Sligo. Shelbourne want to play on Saturday so that they can have the services of Priestley, their International left-winger. Rovers want to play on Sunday so that their supporters can witness the match. That's the crux in a nutshell, and the decision rests with the [FAI] Council, who will meet on Tuesday night next.'

At the protest meeting in Sligo, a compromise idea had been put forward that the game could be played on Easter Monday. However, Mayor Conlon batted the suggestion aside, arguing that such a move would also prove untenable, as the many counter-attractions in Dublin on the bank holiday would seriously impact the expected cup final gate receipts – a potentially lucrative 25 per cent of which would be pocketed by the westerners.

So to conclude the protest gathering, the following resolution was passed on the proposition of Sligo's mayor and the message was sent in no uncertain terms to the FAI Council in Dublin:

'That we, the supporters of Sligo Rovers, submit that the reported application of Shelbourne F.C. to have the date of the Cup final changed should not be considered on the following grounds – (1) That the date of the fixture was officially arranged at a meeting of the Council on 8 June, when Shelbourne's representative was present; (2)

that never before in the history of the Cup was the final played on a Saturday; (3) that provincial clubs depend for 90 per cent of their support from Sunday followers of football.'

The final portion of the resolution presented the FAI Council with Sligo's nuclear option should the date be changed – the withdrawal of the Bit O' Red from the competition and the club's ultimate disbandment.

* * *

The controversy drew reaction from fans across the game, as evidenced from the letters to a number of Dublin papers published in *The Sligo Champion* in the days that followed. Indeed, and probably unsurprisingly, the view in the capital was to suggest that the people of Sligo were going too far – as did some of the comparisons made in the letters to Sligo's threats if they did not get their way! On several occasions, betraying the times and the world in which those writing were living, the pronouncements and demands out of Connacht were unflatteringly compared to happenings in Nazi Germany!

Here's a sample of what the paper received:

> Sir,
>
> I agree with your correspondents who deprecate the Hitler-like action of the Sligo supporters in threatening to disband if they don't get their own way. Surely it was a matter that could have been met in a sporting way by the club, who are very popular in Dublin.

Which will lose most if the match is played on Sunday? Shelbourne will lose the service of their match-winner Priestley, and Sligo will lose nothing. If played on Saturday, Sligo will not lose the services of their match winner, Dixie Dean. Supposing Sligo were, through no fault of theirs or of the player, compelled to play without 'Dixie' on a certain day, would they, too, not ask for a change of date?

Sligo can have a full team on either Saturday or Sunday, but Shelbourne are this season looking to Priestley more than to any other player to win the Cup, and he is the one player who through no fault of his or of his club cannot play on Sunday. As regards support, every soccer fan knows that they [Sligo] will get the cheers of practically every follower of the other Dublin clubs. Do Sligo seriously believe that their followers were the only ones who cheered for them against Dundalk?

Did not at least half of the vast crowd not shout themselves hoarse for the Westerners? Sligo have absolutely no case except that the match was fixed for Sunday. But how many League matches were fixed for certain dates and then subsequently changed? Was not the recent Sligo–St James's Gate League match not changed?

It looks as if Sligo are doing their utmost to take advantage of the Priestley circumstance to meet a weakened Shelbourne team, and they have proved that by threatening to disband if it is played on Easter Monday as an alternative. If this is not so, let Sligo have the match on Sunday, but drop 'Dixie' as a compensation for the absence of Priestley!

Anti-Humbug

Sir,

I have read with amazement Sligo Rovers' 'ultimatum'. Surely the decision could have been left with the FAI Council without these 'Hitler' methods. A few years in senior soccer and they try to dictate to clubs who are the founders of the game in Eire. Shelbourne, if they are not compelled by the FAI rules to play on Sunday, should insist on Saturday. After all, no matter how well a provincial team are playing, they have to depend on the support of the Dublin followers in semi-finals and finals to keep them going. Their 1,000 followers would not take up very much space in a 30,000 gate at Dalymount.

'Cup for Ringsend'

Sir,

Regarding the Cup final, I wish to protest against Sligo's attitude and threat. I always thought that when the final was not played on a Saturday before, it was when Sunday suited both teams. Now it is different, as Shelbourne, like Bohemians, two of the oldest teams in the country, depend on Saturday supporters.

Sligo Rovers would be no loss to the other clubs, but Shelbourne would, as was the case some years ago. Sligo should not be allowed to dictate and use threats to the Council. Their attitude is to try and play Shelbourne without Priestley, the cleverest wing forward in the country, and have an advantage.

Shamrock Rovers Fan

Sir,

I am a Belfast man in Dublin on business and as I take a keen interest in soccer I am interested in the case. In the olden days I saw Shels and Bohs playing many times, and both these teams were Saturday teams. Sligo have a very lame excuse, and I'm wondering if it is the day or Tom Priestley that is worrying them. To be fair to both teams concerned, I would suggest the match be played on Whit Monday May 29th. This date would enable followers from all parts of Ireland.

J.P.

* * *

As Volt's reporting was understandably skewed by his local affiliations, it's interesting to read how the matter was viewed by the Dublin-based *Evening Herald*'s soccer correspondent, NAT. His opinion piece published on the day that the issue was to be ruled upon by the FAI, Wednesday, 5 April, throws more light on the controversy and perhaps took a less partisan outlook. Moreover, it suggested that the Sligo Rovers protest ultimately hardened hearts and opinions in Ringsend when in fact the Dublin side were expected to simply make their case and then ready themselves for a Sunday final.

'It is difficult to anticipate with certainty what will happen. The chairman would be in an invidious and unenvious position if called on to give a ruling. He would have to decide in favour of the Sunday date, which was fixed by last season's Council, whose right to do so might be challenged, or stand by the unwritten law that clubs cannot be compelled to play on the Sabbath. The alternative is to throw the onus of a decision on the meeting.

'No matter how the verdict is given or reached, it seems slight odds on a Sunday final. Shelbourne have taken precautions against that eventuality by signing a new outside right – Drain of Newry Town – to deputise for Priestley, and the move suggests a feeling inside the club that the decision will go against them. At one time it was, in fact, thought in certain quarters that the [Shelbourne] Directors would be content with merely stating their case in a more or less academic manner. Whether the attitude ever existed is a moot point, but there is no doubt now that the Management, who have been told what they are expected to do in letters received from their followers, will press their claim with utmost vigour.

'In higher circles, it is believed that the hasty action of calling a public meeting in Sligo has created an awkward atmosphere for a decision. It is felt by some people in close touch with affairs that the protest was premature or unnecessary, as there was nothing to protest against.

'This phase of the subject is likely, it is understood, to come in for some criticism. But it is hard to see what can be done.

'The meeting was held by the supporters of Sligo, apart from the Club, who may not have had anything to do with the matter at all, and, while they may be blamed for impetuosity, their concern for their own interests cannot be gainsaid.

'My reference last week to a hint that the right to fix the date, 23 April, for the final, in the way it was done, could and might be questioned, has brought requests from correspondents for more clarity to satisfy their curiosity. I was purposely vague because of anxiety to avoid appearing to take sides in a controversy that had two sides. The doubt indicated is whether Cup dates have been made all along contrary to the manner prescribed. Rule 16 implies that they are to be decided on for each round as the draw is made and notified to the clubs concerned. Unless there is an overriding rule somewhere outside the Cup rules, the present practice of deciding on dates in globo and months ahead could hardly be held to be in order. There is no need to follow that view, if sound, to its logical conclusion.

'In any case, everyone will hope that the official decision will be accepted by all in a sporting spirit and care taken that no similar question will arise again.'

* * *

Matters came to a head in a vote held that Wednesday at a meeting of the FAI's Council in which officials of both clubs presented their arguments.

Shelbourne's representative at the Council meeting, T.P. Cullen, stated that this was the first year in which a specific date for the cup final had been set down. In previous seasons, a weekend was earmarked and a decision on the actual day agreed upon by the clubs and the Association.

Cullen argued that it was an 'established precedent' that if a club wanted to play on a Saturday they could not be compelled to play on a Sunday.

The Shelbourne man laid out three key reasons why his side wished to play on Saturday: firstly, they were most definitely a Saturday team; secondly, their supporters wanted it on a Saturday; and thirdly, they could only field a full team on a Saturday.

He concluded his remarks by warning that if Sunday were decided upon, it would be the first time a club had been forced to play on a particular day and the Council would have to take the consequences for such a decision.

The Bit O' Red's representative (Mr A. McCabe) responded, stating that as Saturday was the busiest day in Sligo, it being market day, very few of the team's supporters from the town or the county would be able to travel to the final in Dublin (some 110 miles away – no easy distance on the roads of 1930s Ireland).

The case went to a Council vote, which the westerners won by a count of 14 to eight. And so it was confirmed that the FAI Cup Final would be played as originally planned on Sunday, 23 April, much to the delight of all involved with the Connacht club.

What impact Sligo's strong stance may have had on the decision will probably never be known, although the Football Association's chairman, Mr T. Hutchinson, made the organisation's feelings clear about the westerners' threat in a statement following the vote.

Referring to the protest meeting held in Sligo the previous week, Hutchinson said 'it was to be deplored that when people desire to put forward a case for any particular cause that the case should be accompanied by threats'. He added that he would like to assure all concerned that 'the Council would not be influenced by threats from clubs, sections of the public, or views expressed at a public meeting'. The admonishment aside, it was, nevertheless, a major result for the Sligo club. Their fans would be free to travel in numbers to the club's first-ever appearance in an FAI Cup Final. Moreover, they would be facing a Shelbourne side deprived of its most influential and creative performer.

The reaction of the westerners' to the mooted switch may well have been heavy-handed and perhaps a little melodramatic; however, had they not made those threats and made such a passionate defence of their position, could they have found themselves playing on the Saturday instead? And regardless of how disgruntled their opponents may have felt, it is surely fair to say that had the game been switched, it would have been to accommodate just the one man – the aforementioned Priestley – at the expense of many thousands of others.

Depriving the Sligo Rovers fans of the opportunity of travelling to Dublin for such an historic occasion for the club and the town would surely not have been in the spirit of the game.

* * *

Meanwhile, amidst the hullabaloo and hot air, the Bit O' Red and Dixie Dean still had football matches to attend to. In fact, in a weekend that would have modern-day player welfare representatives taking to the airwaves in alarm, Rovers returned to Dublin the weekend after their FAI Cup semi-final triumph for a double-header on Saturday, 1 April and Sunday, 2 April against St James's Gate and champions in waiting Shamrock Rovers, respectively.

As it happened, Dean missed the Iveagh Grounds game with the Gate – an ultimately inglorious affair that saw the westerners play the majority of the second half with just ten men, shipping three goals in the process. The less said the better about that game, even now.

The following day, however, Dean was back as the westerners visited Milltown to face Shamrock Rovers, a day on which the Dublin side were to be crowned champions – becoming the first side in the league's history to retain the title. The game itself ended three apiece – a six-goal thriller, in which Dixie figured prominently, that gave the Hoops the point they ultimately needed to secure top spot. At the start of play, their nearest rivals, Dundalk, still had an outside chance of catching them. However, a surprising draw at home in Oriel Park to struggling Drumcondra put paid to their slim hopes, making the gap between the Lilywhites and the Dublin side mathematically unbridgeable.

Shamrock Rovers' Milltown coronation was an end-to-end affair that showcased the attacking prowess of both the Hoops and Sligo Rovers and the fighting spirit that made the Dubliners deserved champions. Their thrilling comeback from being 3-1 down to Dean and co early in the second half underlined their never-say-die attitude. And although Dixie failed to find the back of the net on this occasion, he did wow the big Dublin crowd with another eye-catching display, rattling the home side's bar, creating numerous chances and setting up two of his side's goals.

Losing a two-goal lead may have been a disappointment for the visitors, but at least the weekend had ended better than it had started for Sligo. And there was an added bonus – Dundalk's dropped point had not only handed Shamrock Rovers the league, but it had also given the westerners renewed hope of securing the more than respectable league runners-up spot with just three games to go.

12

Goals and Golf as Dixie Prospers

EASTER SUNDAY saw Sligo Rovers close in on the League of Ireland runners-up position with a resounding 6-1 victory over visiting strugglers Brideville. The side hailing from Dublin's Liberties were no match for their slicker provincial opponents, but Rovers will have taken a deal of satisfaction from the result all the same, not only for the goals notched and the points they garnered, but also because of the intimidatory manner in which the Dubliners approached the game. Moreover, the fact that Dundalk dropped another point in the chase for second spot, this time at Shelbourne, just added to their sense of contentment.

Robust would be a kind characterisation of the style employed by the visitors, as Brideville got stuck into the westerners from the off, much to the consternation of the Bit O' Red's players, support and the watching *Sligo Champion* reporter. 'The first half of the game gave no indication of the fireworks that were to follow in the second half. Fireworks they were and not of the type that do credit to Association football, but I should hasten to add that they were not caused by the Sligo team. Rovers offered a passive resistance to over-keen tackling by the Brideville players, and the fact that they held their tempers speaks well for them.'

Indeed, tempers simmered and then flared, the result of a disputed penalty awarded to the home side, after the visitors had dragged themselves back into the game just after half-time.

Rovers had led comfortably 2-0 at the break and appeared content to rest on their laurels given the somewhat relaxed fashion in which they had started the second period. Sensing the drop in intensity, Brideville grabbed one back on 50 minutes and clearly believed that an unlikely draw was possible. But the home side were awarded the hotly disputed penalty not long after. According to the *Champion*'s match report, had the visitors held their tempers and their composure, there was still a strong chance that they could have salvaged something from the afternoon – but instead, they lost their heads; throwing 'all construction to the winds', they seemed to lose interest in the ball and lost two of their number to red cards in a bad-tempered second half.

Right-half William Hay, formerly of Leicester City, was the Showgrounds hero, bagging a hat-trick of penalties on the day, while Seddon, Johnston and Dean also pitched in with goals. Indeed, it was a surprise that Dean didn't score more in what was said to be another classy display – testing the Brideville keeper on a number of occasions with trademark headed efforts and hitting the bar.

But despite the convincing nature of the win, the home fans clearly felt no level of sympathy for the vanquished visitors – so unpleasant and agricultural had their approach been to the game. And perhaps still harbouring some of the militancy witnessed during the public protests and threats over the possible switching of the FAI Cup Final date, many of them invaded the pitch on the referee's final whistle to remonstrate with the Brideville players and let them know in no uncertain terms just how dimly they viewed their overly physical efforts.

* * *

For Dixie Dean himself, it had been quite the sporting weekend, for he had played the Brideville game shortly after competing in the third round of the West of Ireland Golf Championships! Indeed, he had been knocked out of the renowned match play tournament, which was open to golf club professionals and useful amateurs, that very morning! (The competition has long been a proving ground for Irish golfing talent – with golf major winners Rory McIlroy, Padraig Harrington and Shane Lowry all having won the tournament in their fledgling careers.)

Dean had been an avid golfer since his teens back in Birkenhead and had long been a scratch player. According to Nick Walsh's book, Dixie's first taste of the game had come when he picked up a caddying job at the age of 12 at the Wirral Ladies Golf Club. Young Dean had pitched up at the course with the aim of earning a few coppers of pocket money. But the amenable members had allowed him to practise and play a bit, and it was perhaps unsurprising that he took to the game almost immediately.

'The caddying job presented him with many opportunities he would not otherwise have had to practise the game of golf,' wrote Walsh. 'As an engine driver's son, particularly in those days, he could scarcely have afforded to take up the sport seriously, but in the circumstances, he lost no opportunity to develop his game. Dean was a natural in the sense that he possessed, even as a boy, all the physical and mental attributes which enabled him to acquire a high standard of skill at any ball game ... By the time Dean was 15 years of age his golf handicap was down to two strokes.'

Doubtless had he decided on golf rather than football as his game, Dean would've been just as successful given his apparent aptitude for all things sporting. Just one of those annoying people who seem to be naturally good at every sport they try their hand at, it would seem!

Dixie's golf game continued to improve after becoming a professional footballer, affording him plenty of time to hone his skills. And by the time he was 20 and lining out for Everton, Walsh tells us that Dixie 'was a scratch player and was successful in a number of tournaments arranged for professional footballers. Indeed, he won the Wirral Amateur Golf Championships.'

So perhaps it was little surprise that with time on his hands in that Sligo spring, Dean fancied his chances in the prestigious locally staged tournament, the more so given it was to be played at the stunning County Sligo Golf Club links course at Rosses Point with which he had already become familiar and had grown to love.

Dean had been known to frequent the links on afternoons or days off – and his knowledge of the course clearly gave him something of an edge.[9] The tournament began on Saturday, 8 April, with the first two rounds played that day. Dean, who as ever drew a large crowd of onlookers, squeezed by Malone Golf Club's P. Bryan on the last hole in the morning, before defeating Major Martin of Foxrock more easily, four and three, that afternoon.

Easter Sunday was to feature just the one round, which was just as well, as Dean was set to line out in the Showgrounds at 3.30 that afternoon against Brideville. Unfortunately for the star attraction and the big galleries that were drawn to him, Dixie bowed out, losing three and one to W. Smyth of Royal County Down.

According to the brief report in *The Sligo Champion*, the Bit O' Red's hitman had impressed during his first two matches and surely 'would have gone into the fourth round had he been on better terms with his putter'. Thankfully for Sligo Rovers, however, he was as clinical

---

9 Little is known of or reported on Dixie's movements in Ireland when not playing football. Golf was certainly one way in which he filled his time. And according to his granddaughter, Melanie, his love of horse racing and boxing meant it was highly likely that he would have sought out local race meetings or fights to pass the time. He was also, she said, not averse to the odd pint and was known to have been more than happy to share a drink with the locals – his highly social nature serving to help him bed in well with his generous Sligo hosts.

as ever on the football field later that day, helping the club edge ever closer to securing second place in the League of Ireland championship.

* * *

The following Sunday, Sligo Rovers finished out their home league fixtures with the visit of Bray Unknowns. The home side were without McDaid, Johnston and Seddon and played well within themselves. With the FAI Cup Final only a week away, it was perhaps unsurprising that there was, as Volt noted, a 'certain amount of carefulness in Rovers' play', although he felt that that alone 'could not excuse their weakness in finishing off movements'. Indeed, Rovers made enough chances in the first 45 minutes, according to his report, to 'win three games', but they failed to take any of them.

Thankfully, in the second half, Dean shook them out of their torpor and scored the opener on the hour mark, pouncing on Hay's cross to give them the lead. And it was Dean again who put the game beyond the Wicklow side, nodding home Began's cross to make it two. Dixie was looking a different animal now – fitter, more mobile, sharper – to the player who struggled somewhat back in February when the two sides first met in Ringsend.

The Unknowns did pull one back, but Rovers held on comfortably for the two points – and as the final whistle blew, all attention turned to Dalymount Park and the build-up for the cup final, which was now just a week away.

13

Dalymount Beckons

THERE WAS high excitement in the county as Sligo Rovers' first-ever cup final hove into view. The furthest the club had ever progressed in the competition was to the semi-finals four years earlier – in Sligo's first season in senior football – falling at the feet of Dundalk in front of a crowd of some 20,000 at Dalymount Park. But the decider with Shelbourne was expected to draw an even bigger number, a point underscored by the more than healthy sales of railway and stand tickets for the day, which suggested a record exodus from the west for a football match.

Financially, the FAI Cup Final would be a huge boost to both clubs. The FAI itself was set to take 50 per cent of the gate when all expenses were paid, with the two finalists sharing the other 50. And for the winner, the extra bonus of £100 (€7,000). But for both sides, this final meant so much more – given neither had ever brought the cup home. Shels had come the closer – losing twice in the final to the now long-forgotten Alton United from the Falls Road in Belfast in 1923 and to Shamrock Rovers in 1925.

Sligo Rovers fans, according to *The Sligo Champion*, were confident that the cup would be travelling west of the Shannon for the first time. Volt, in his preview of the game, argued that there were very good grounds for optimism. For him, Shelbourne's struggles against the likes of Bray Unknowns and St James's Gate in previous rounds suggested that the Ringsend outfit were not a particularly strong side. And the fact that Rovers had come out on top in two of the three meetings between the sides that season – in the Shield back in August and again in the league on Dean's debut in late January – strengthened that optimistic air.

And so too did the fact that Shelbourne's talismanic wide man Tom Priestley would not be available. Volt did pose a note or two of caution, however, and felt that the Dubliners were strong in the middle of the park where 'Sharkey is constructive, and [Bill] Little, who is a bustling type of pivot, can be counted upon to watch Dean keenly'. But it was Scottish inside-right Alexander Weir who concerned the Sligo reporter the most – labelling him one of the best in that position in the country. But if he could be 'mastered', then the Bit O' Red would be going 'a long way in taking the sting out of the Dublin side's attack'. Volt also discussed how the weekend could prove a massive vindication for the Sligo Rovers committee who had made no secret of their desire to win the FAI Cup and had made a massive statement of intent, some said a massive gamble, in signing Dixie Dean just before the competition started. Indeed, the great centre-forward had been Sligo's most influential player in the previous rounds and would have been especially deserving of a winner's medal. 'All eyes at Dalymount on Sunday will be centred on the man who beat the famous Steve Bloomer's English goalscoring record of 352 League goals in September 1936.' Incredibly, that was just three seasons before. A long time in football, of course, but not so long that Dean had slipped into obscurity.

Indeed, such was his status that a large crowd from his home city were expected to attend the game – largely made up of merchant sailors who manned the many ships that traded between Dublin and Liverpool. 'To the Merseyside sailors,' Volt wrote, 'Dean is still their idol.'

And one other omen offered positive portents – Sligo Rovers had won the toss for colours and would play in their famous red, with Shels bedecked in unfamiliar blue.

The Sligo Champion's big-game preview also reported that Sligo's captain and player-coach Alf Peachey was confident of victory and that his side were 'fighting fit' having trained at Strandhill over the week, playing matches on the beach and even swimming. Some had also taken to the waters of Lough Gill for a day of rowing before all eased off with some light training sessions on the Friday and Saturday.

Rovers were ready to roll. And to further add to the sense of occasion and excitement, in the run-up to the big day, the paper printed a number of FAI Cup Final songs penned by local fans to help get everyone in the mood. Below are just two of the ditties – how could the men from the west fail to be inspired!

In a letter to the paper, the correspondent 'PJ' suggested that the following song, sung to the air of 'Daisy', might inspire Dean and his team-mates at Dalymount Park:

> Dixie, Dixie, give us a hat-trick, do:
> Poor old Shelbourne, your chance is looking blue,
> When Peachey blots his man out
> You'll hear the Rovers' fans shout:
> 'The Reds are up
> To lift the cup
> And we'll fill it with champagne too!'

And if that didn't do the trick, then the following rousing tune to the air of 'The Chestnut Tree' might well get the Bit O' Red over the line:

> Underneath the bar, to Shelbourne's net,
> The Reds will hang the ball–don't fret
> When Peachey and his wing halves get all set
> Past the lines the Blues won't get
> Show these boys from Dublin
> The West is mighty tough.
> 'Gee whiz!' the fizz is bubblin'
> Come on Reds, do your stuff!
> Underneath the bar poor Webster stands,
> Trembling knees and outstretched hands;

While into the net—another lands—
'The Cup is ours' yell Rovers' fans!

Chas and Dave, eat your heart out!

* * *

Big-match previews in the other Irish newspapers make for interesting reading. The *Irish Press*'s Socaro also felt that Dean's team were favourites to lift the cup, being 'the better-balanced side'. The greater subtlety and creativity in the Sligo Rovers ranks would likely give them the edge.

Socaro felt that Dean's presence could be key. He was sure to be closely policed by the Shelbourne captain, Bill Little, amongst others, but the necessary guarding against the threat he posed was likely to open up space for the other Rovers forwards and give them the 'chance to indulge in rapier-like thrusts, which may produce a match winner'. That said, the *Irish Press*'s man was well aware of the Englishman's ability to produce a match-winner of his own. 'Dean, even if he fails to get an opportunity to send in his bullet-like drives, is very dangerous with his head, and so [John] Webster [the Shelbourne keeper] will have an anxious time when "Dixie" is in his vicinity.'

The *Cork Examiner*'s preview was a little more on the fence about the ultimate outcome but did suggest that the cup final experience of two of Shelbourne's veterans could play a part – portentously, as it turned out, in the case of one of the named combatants.

'If Sligo win the Cup their players will receive their first medals, but the honour, if the Cup stays in Dublin, will be no novelty to some of the Shelbourne players. That grand old veteran, Liam "Sacky" Glen, won a runners-up medal with Shamrock Rovers the first year the Cup was won by St James's Gate way back in 1922. He has since gained 7 Cup medals and 2 runners-up medals, not to mention his League and Shield medals. [David] "Babby" Byrne is almost as much a veteran as Glen and has won four Cup medals with Shamrock Rovers.'

But for the *Examiner*, it was a final that really could go either way. The side best able to impose themselves would be the most likely winners.

'If Sligo can make a football game out of it, the Cup should go West, but if Shelbourne are good enough to dictate their own play to the Westerners, then Shelbourne might bring it off.' Bets were duly hedged.

The *Evening Herald*'s NAT also had his say on the likely outcome, but not before he talked about the pulling power of this edition of the FAI Cup Final, which, to the surprise of some (mainly in the capital), looked like drawing record gate receipts.

'The belief that the fight for football's most cherished prize would lose its glamour and pulling power if successful giants of the past were not participating has been refuted by the remarkable wave of enthusiasm that has swept the metropolis and provinces on this occasion.'

NAT reported that within a week of the tickets for the reserved stand (the only seated area in Dalymount Park right up to the 1990s) being made available, they were sold out, and the demand was not even close to being half met. Moreover, bookings on the special trains coming from Belfast, Cork, Limerick and Sligo suggested that the attendance would push the 30,000 mark and possibly go beyond.

'That the Cup final maintains its popularity and grip in all and any circumstances is illustrated,' wrote NAT, 'by the change of views and feelings that has taken place amongst the crowds. A few weeks ago, after the form had been revealed in the semi-finals, comment was cold. Now the fervour of the fans has boiled over spontaneously to such an extent that the receipts record is confidently expected to be touched, if not exceeded.'

NAT also noted another interesting trend in the weeks leading up to the final – a gradual shift in views that had at one stage seen Sligo Rovers as clear favourites but that had subsequently 'wheeled round to the extent that Shelbourne are now regarded as having equal chance'. Improving form in the weeks before the Dalymount clash played a part in the change of thinking with regards to the Dublin side. As had the fact that they had appeared to grow stronger through the rounds and found a way to win in seeing off cup holders St James's Gate in round one, an obdurate Bray Unknowns at the third attempt and then impressively besting Dublin rivals Bohemians, albeit only 1-0, in the semi-final at Milltown. Their 'disconcerting way of pulling off a coup', as NAT put it, had many observers suggesting that this could well be their year.

Turning his attention to Dean's side, NAT noted that, like their opponents, Sligo Rovers had their own fair share of luck in reaching the final. But their decision to focus all resources on the competition had every chance of paying off. 'Sligo have landed into the final after five years in the senior ranks and have accomplished all they expected and for which they had planned. They, in short, have concentrated this season on the Cup and will be keenly disappointed if they fall at the last fence.'

However, the *Evening Herald*'s correspondent wasn't particularly impressed with the westerners' displays on route to the Phibsborough final: 'They did not achieve much in beating Cork City to get on the upward trail, and a subsequent narrow victory over Leinster Leaguers, Distillery, could not have created optimism.' And 'they won the semi-final because of the help they got from Dundalk'. Doubtless Volt would have taken issue with such a jaundiced view!

NAT tended to agree with the other correspondents in terms of the Bit O' Red's greater fluidity and the superior quality of their football; however, he did feel that they often played to a plan from which they seldom strayed. He argued that such rigidity in a one-off game where 'initiative is telling' could be their downfall.

On Dixie Dean, NAT spared a short paragraph. 'It is obvious that Dean is expected to play a prominent part, even if only in the fact that he is someone that needs close watching and also for the steadying influence he can operate.' A counterbalance to the cup final experience of Glen and Byrne, you might say.

However, the *Herald*'s man, like Socaro in the *Irish Press*, felt it was another Englishman in the Sligo Rovers eleven who was likely to exert the greatest influence on the Bit O' Red's cup final fortunes – centre-half Alfred Peachey.

Peachey, who hailed from St Helens on Merseyside, only 12 miles from Dean's Birkenhead home, had arrived at the start of the season, after ten years with Bradford City, as Sligo's player-coach. The 31-year-old had a decade of experience in English Division Two and had been a standout performer with the westerners that season. His ability to step out with the ball from deep positions into midfield and make the play had caught many an eye and saw him represent the League of Ireland with distinction against the Scottish and Northern Irish leagues already that season.

For both football writers, Peachey was key. Making the Sligo Rovers defender sound a touch Franz Beckenbauer, NAT praised his ability 'to take a hand in attack without impairing his undoubted defensive abilities'. Socaro was similarly effusive. 'Peachey is their key player. There is no need to elaborate on his ability. He proved his worth against the cream of Scottish football, and as he is much more than the "stopper" type of centre-half, he may well dominate the midfield. His well-directed passes to his inside forwards, O'Connor and Johnston, puts the Sligo attack in machine-like motion.'

The reference to the 'cream of Scottish football' relates to the first-ever meeting of the League of Ireland selection and their Scottish counterparts on St Patrick's Day in Dalymount Park a few weeks previously. Peachey, along with his Rovers team-mate Johnston, had shone as the home side beat their illustrious visitors 2-1 in front of a crowd of 35,000.

So, in short, according to the two Dublin-based correspondents, if Shelbourne could stop Peachey and Dean, then the Ringsend side had a serious chance of coming out on top.

For Spectator, the soccer correspondent in the Cork-based newspaper the *Evening Echo*, Shelbourne's ability to deal with the threat posed by Sligo's former English international centre-forward would likely decide the tie. 'Can Shelbourne put a stopper on Dixie Dean?' he wondered. 'If they can, they will have more than half-won the trophy for the first time in the history of the club. That is the crux of the whole matter—Dixie Dean. He alone will win or lose the Cup for Sligo.'

For the *Echo*'s correspondent, Rovers, known for the style of their attacking play, had stepped things up a level since Dixie's arrival in January. The Bit O' Red's forward line now played with a greater cohesion, inspired and directed by Dean's experience, his ability to read the game and his creativity.

'If Shels can hold the famous centre-forward, the defence should have an easier task in subduing Began, O'Connor, Monaghan and McPeake, for without the master touch that their leader is capable of giving, the Sligo forwards may play a comparatively aimless game. That word "comparatively" there means a lot. Before Dixie ever donned Irish football boots, Sligo Rovers had made a name for themselves from their stylish forward play. Even without Dixie, the skill and dash of those Sligo sharpshooters would probably have been enough to keep the team well up in the league table. Since the arrival of Dean, the forward line has developed from sound to brilliant, and today ranks as one of the most dangerous in the country. With Dixie bottled, Sligo would lose much of their efficiency in attack, and while they may still prove too good for the Shelbourne defenders, even without the help of the Englishman, Shels will have an infinitely easier task than they would if they fail to hold Dixie Dean.'

Spectator noted, however, that Shelbourne had been preparing for the final with Dean very much on their minds. 'Shels fully realise what they are up against in Dean and their preparations and training have been aimed at a standard that would match all the science and wizardry of the Everton star.'

But as with Socaro, Spectator felt that too much of a focus on Dean could spell danger for the Ringsend side. And then again, a failure to give him the respect he deserved could be equally problematic for the Shels.

'I don't believe there is any single man in Shelbourne that could hold Dean by himself. That job will take at least a couple of men, and if a couple of men are delegated to the task, the rest of the defence will be in a rather weakened condition, numerically, at any rate. That would suit Sligo's book nicely. So, no matter what tactic Shels adopt, they would seem to be in a cleft stick.'

Spectator's conclusion? That the Sligo Rovers committee had pulled off a great coup in bringing Dean to Ireland and were set to reap a rather fine dividend.

'Sligo did a good day's work when they signed Dean. He has brought them into the final of the Cup already and now it looks as if he will win it for them for the first time in their history.'

14

The 1939 FAI Cup Final

ON FAI Cup Final morning, fans were up early and already streaming to Sligo station by eight o'clock – chattering excitedly, with the odd song along the way, bedecked in red and white, many with rattles and bells, waking those who were not already conscious along the way.

Many among the throng had been saving up for weeks for the occasion, hoarding the sixpences to 'make' the fare – men, women and children making their way to the trains laid on for the exodus and the long trip to the east coast and the capital. According to the unnamed *Sligo Champion* reporter embedded with the fans, such was the migration that a milkman he met on the way to the station told him that 'his Saturday night accounts had dwindled into insignificance, but he seemed cheerful enough about it'. The *Champion*'s colour piece, printed the Saturday after the final, painted the picture beautifully of Sligo's first FAI Cup Final.

'The first long train was already crammed with humanity, and off it went. The second filled up rapidly and then it too rumbled out of the station bearing its load of Cup-confident supporters. On the road there were buses and cars, some of them with red and white flags at their mudguards, all their bonnets directed towards Dalymount Park, Mecca of the Soccer fan.

'Into Amiens Street station came the last special and down the dungeon-like steps to the street poured the fans. "Wish we had those traffic lights in Sligo" remarks one, gazing with interest at Dublin's automatic pointsmen. Then the crowd from Sligo spread over the city for food, and soon after, they were crowding into trams Phibsborough-bound. Some of them took sidecars and they made O'Connell Street lively with "The West's Awake", sung in several keys. Shelbourne's supporters had an aggrieved look as they wore their new colours – blue and red, having to give way to Sligo, who also play in scarlet.

'The crowd became more dense in the large space fronting Dalymount Park and the turnstiles clicked continuously. Inside the ground St. James's brass and reed band were taking turns with the Fintan Lawlor pipe band in entertaining the spectators. There was a continuous movement along the embankments and to the stands. The crowd had not yet solidified into a black and white mass, and so those moving on the stand made a thunder for the ears of the players in the dressing rooms below.'

The *Champion*'s intrepid reporter had access to the Sligo Rovers dressing room and observed the following preparations: 'I found Dixie tying a last knot on his football boots, cool and unexcited. A player who has heard the terrific roar of Hampden as he scored the winning goal for England is unlikely to feel "nerves" before a Dalymount crowd. Peachey, the captain, looked as fit as anyone could possibly be, talking quietly to each player in turn. Before all matches there are jokes in the dressing room; before this match players were even more apparently light-hearted, concealing the tension they felt with laughter.'

Our correspondent then headed to the press box to take his match position in time to see the teams emerge from the tunnel. 'Sligo were first out, cameras clicked and the crowd roared, and they roared again as Shelbourne appeared. A cameraman exploded with rage as someone wandered in front of his lens, deaf to the entreaties shouted at him amidst the uproar.

'In the centre of the pitch, the band played the national anthem while the crowd and the players stood to attention. At its conclusion, there was a roar which had in it some of the thrilling anticipation that makes every true fan's heart beat a little faster before each important game. In time for the start, a crowd of Sligo's supporters file into their seats on the "A" stand. Their bus had engine trouble at Enfield, and a phone call to the city requisitioned another bus in which they completed their journey. They had nothing to eat since 6.30 that morning, but they did not appear greatly worried.

'Rovers had three mascots who toddled onto the pitch in red and white. Shelbourne's mascot was a little girl who shyly shook hands with Peachey and Little, Shels' captain. Dressed entirely in suits of blue, four Shelbourne fans rushed out to present Webster with a dozen horseshoes, and Cranston received more good-luck charms at his end.'

* * *

Events on the pitch after referee Mr Hartles, who had travelled over from Runcorn in England to officiate, set the game in motion were captured by Volt in his match report.

'Thousands of Sligo Rovers' supporters cheered their team in the first half of the FAI Cup Final at Dalymount Park last Sunday, as they watched them over-run Shelbourne. In the second half, those supporters held their breath and watched the second hands of their watches as Shelbourne became transformed into a storming combination, equalised, and almost snatched the Cup from Rovers' grasp.

'It was a typical Cup final; all the escapes, mistakes and misses were there. Dogged defences that sometimes made slips, forwards who did extraordinarily clever things and then missed the easiest of chances. Shelbourne's phenomenal luck in this year's Cup competition still held good. By all the unwritten rules of football, Sligo Rovers should have returned triumphantly with the Cup; instead, the teams will have to meet next Wednesday, 3 May at the same venue.

'It will be remembered as a game in which Sligo's forwards failed. Behind them they had halves and backs who played themselves to a standstill, working through the 90 minutes as if their lives depended on getting the ball up to the attack. At the end of the first half, Sligo should have led by three goals, in the second they were lucky to have held out as Shelbourne forced a replay.

'Once again Dixie Dean carried the Bit O' Red upon his broad shoulders. From the first round to the final, he has brought the team through. On Sunday, he scored the all-important goal and handed goals on a plate to each of the other forwards, particularly [Hugh] O'Connor, who missed opportunities Sligo's diminutive mascot would have turned to account. Making allowance for the excitement and the strain of a final game, Rovers' inside right's mistakes were seemingly inexcusable.

'Once he ballooned the ball over the bar from four yards with Webster out of position, and, shortly afterwards, he sent wide when confronted with an open goal. It was all the more tragic for O'Connor that apart from his misses he was a hard-working, clever inside right.'

As ever, it was the former Everton star Dean who caught Volt's eye as he tormented the Shelbourne defence in the first period.

The great striker had a headed goal disallowed after clever play by Monaghan and Johnston down the left. Then came the two glaring misses from O'Connor – the first clearing the crossbar from close range with Shelbourne's keeper Webster down on one knee. The second was worse just a minute later. 'Dean sidestepped and then beat Little and did everything to make a goal except push O'Connor's boot against the ball. O'Connor shot wildly and sliced the ball yards wide' of the gaping goal.

Finally, however, the goal Sligo's slick attacking play deserved came, with Dean taking matters into his own hands – or rather, taking them unerringly on his head.

'Three minutes from the interval, Johnston sent in a shot from 15 yards; Webster sprang to catch the ball, but with a quick flick Dean sent it flying from his head into the net out of the goalie's reach.'

The goal was met with a deafening clamour: 'Rovers swarmed up to hug Dean and Johnston, while bells, rattles and roars went up to make a Sligo-made pandemonium.' Dean's goal made him the first player ever to score in both the FA and FAI Cup finals. Indeed, only another England great, Raich Carter, has ever done likewise – matching Dean's feat scoring for Cork Athletic in the 1953 replay against Evergreen having scored for Sunderland in the 1937 FA Cup Final at Wembley.

On the terraces and in the stands, 'Rovers' fans hugged and thumped one another, and programmes went flying in the air. Bags of confetti thrown from the top of the stand seats showered on the heads of those below.'

Shelbourne had really struggled to cope with their opponents, playing in that first half 'without method' and displaying a lack of 'cuteness and cleverness' that made disappointment seem inevitable. They were mightily glad to get back into the dressing rooms to regroup when Mr Hartles called time on the first half. They knew that they had been lucky not to be out of the game at that stage, such was Sligo's dominance.

Before the second half had even begun, Dean was again centre of attention. Spotting a female supporter in the crowd who had fainted on the packed terrace, he helped the St John's Ambulance men get the lady out of the crush for some treatment. The man was not just a hero, he had become a superhero!

But back to the game and a second half almost in complete contrast to the first. Shelbourne played like men possessed, roared on by their big support in the 30,000 crowd. This time it was Rovers whose backs were against the wall – ruing, in great football cliché fashion, those missed first-half chances – as their slender lead looked increasingly tenuous.

The tension was unbearable, as the Ringsend side pushed and pushed, and finally drew level with the westerners just 11 minutes from glory.

Shelbourne's Smythe, a tricky left-winger 'with the appearance of a schoolboy', won a corner off McDaid as the clock ticked down. The curly-haired wide man took it beautifully, and in a mess of red and blue, Cranston appeared to lose the flight of the ball and was unable to do much more than help it on its way under the angle of bar and post and agonisingly into the goal. Smythe wheeled away in celebration, joined by his ecstatic team-mates, as the Dublin fans erupted with delight and relief.

Sligo Rovers were rocked on their heels, and as they reeled, the Shelbourne fans and players clearly smelled blood, sensing the opportunity for a famous comeback win. As the men in blue turned up the heat, the westerners struggled to get out of their own half. Their front line, so impressive in the first 45 minutes, had melted away, unable to hold the ball up and take pressure off their defence, where Peachey put up a terrific rearguard action to keep the Rovers in with a shout.

In the last five minutes, Sligo's Monaghan and Shelbourne's Drain both had chances to nick it, but both failed to convert. And as Mr Hartles called time, it was Dean's Sligo who were the happier this time to hear the whistle.

'On to the pitch flowed the crowds,' wrote Volt, 'Smythe was raised to the shoulders of the jubilant Shelbourne fans, and Mr Joseph Wickham, Secretary of the Football Association of Ireland, carefully took the Cup back to a safe place in the Association.

'It was some time before Sligo's supporters realised that the Cup had been within their grasp and had been snatched away. "If" was the most frequently used word on the trains that brought them home. The un-lit bonfires that were set in readiness for the signal of victory stood forlornly in Lord Edward Street, but when the replay takes place, they will be rebuilt again. Pessimism was never a characteristic of Sligo's supporters.' Volt's summary of events was backed up by the reporters of the other main papers present, proving it wasn't a one-eyed, home-town view. This was a game that Sligo Rovers should have had comfortably won by half-time.

The *Irish Press* headline focused on how the westerners lacked the conviction to see the game through. '**The Big**

"Crack Up": Sligo Had the Cup In Their Pockets,' shouted their headline. 'No replay of the Cup would have been necessary on May 3,' wrote Socaro, 'if only Sligo had accepted their chances at Dalymount Park yesterday. The Westerners, who had Shelbourne on the run, should have had the Cup as good as won after the first 45 minutes.'

NAT in the *Evening Herald* concurred, suggesting that the Bit O' Red had more or less run out of gas in the second period and could consider themselves lucky not to have blown it altogether in the last few minutes of the match. 'Sligo Rovers could only get one goal when three, at least, were their due on opportunities and territorial superiority in the first half. In the second period Shelbourne monopolised the attack, but did not get the same chances, though after they obtained a late equaliser, they got complete mastery over the Westerners, who were literally all in, and were saved by time from possible defeat.'

WPM in the *Irish Independent* was very much in tune with the reporting fraternity. Sligo Rovers were the better football team, but they paid dearly for failing to capitalise on their superiority. 'On the run of play, Sligo should have had the game won at the interval. It was not so much a game of football as a siege of the Shelbourne goal for the first forty-five minutes, and only the brilliant keeping of Webster, the gallant work of Glen and Little, and the rank bad shooting of their opponents on a number of occasions saved them from falling into arrears until three minutes before the interval. Sligo did everything but score goals and for a Cup final, their football was very good.'

All also concurred that Dixie Dean had put on an impressive performance and deserved better on the day from his misfiring team-mates.

'Dean gave his best display since coming to Ireland,' wrote Socaro, 'his scheming in the front line was masterly in the first half.' Both NAT and WPM felt that Dixie looked leaner and fitter than they'd seen him during his time in Irish football, which probably informed NAT's assertion that 'Dean did more work in this game than in all of the others he has appeared in.' The Dublin scribblers weren't always as glowing in their reporting on Dean as their *Sligo Champion* counterpart, Volt, although their criticisms tended to revolve around his lack of mobility. That said, his quality was never questioned – and it was very much on show in the first half at Dalymount Park, as Dixie scored one, had another controversially chalked off for offside, tested Webster between the sticks for Shelbourne on a number of occasions and created a series of good opportunities for his colleagues.

But well as Dean played, prompted and probed, the reports on the cup final suggested that it was the parts played by Webster and Dixie's unfortunate club mate O'Connor that were most influential on the final result.

For Shelbourne's keeper, Webster, it was a day to remember. Across the board, those reporting on the game remarked on a brilliant display that kept Shelbourne's hopes alive. And for the hapless O'Connor, it was a day to forget.

'No one should really be surprised at almost anything that occurs or doesn't happen in cup finals,' wrote NAT in the *Evening Herald*, 'but few could be so phlegmatic as not to be amazed by the mystery of the two misses of O'Connor for Sligo in the first half before they took the lead.

'How he hooked the ball over the bar on that first occasion there's no telling. It seemed impossible, as he was almost under the bar. He was not so close on the second occasion, yet still sent the ball wide of an open goal.'

The *Irish Independent*'s WPM could only surmise that the player 'must have put on the wrong boots. To this player fell the best chance of winning the Cup for his side, but he muffed two of the easiest chances he will ever get.'

And to add insult to injury, the poor lad had also suffered the heartache of seeing the overworked Webster push another of his efforts on to the upright. Fine margins. On another day, Hugh O'Connor could have been the hero – the man credited with taking the FAI Cup west of the Shannon and to Sligo for the first time. Instead, he had a day to forget.

* * *

How Dixie Dean saw it all has been lost to the sands of time. But he must surely have reflected as the team returned to Sligo on how close the club had been to glory and how if they could have held on for those last ten minutes, it would have been his goal that had proven decisive. What a fairy tale that would have been for the club and the townspeople ... and for the player who only months before must have believed that his days of glory were days past.

And should he have had any doubts about how important the cup final was to both clubs, to both sets of players and perhaps, more importantly, to both sets of fans and the communities from which each side was spawned, they will have been dispelled the moment the two the sides emerged from under the reserved stand for the prematch rituals and pleasantries.

Dalymount Park, with its three banked terraces and small wooden-seated stand, may not have had the grand scale of Goodison Park or Wembley, but the tumult and the vibrancy as the match got underway in earnest will have been every bit as visceral. The Phibsborough ground in its heyday, when it was often filled to bursting, was both an intimidating and an inspiring place to perform. As with many such grounds of the time, and certainly the most atmospheric ones, the paying public were not just on top of each other, but they were almost on top of the players to boot!

The attendance on the day of 30,651 was just £53 (€3,800) less than the record FAI Cup Final attendance from two seasons previous, when Shamrock Rovers beat Cork City. The days when the old ground was allowed such a crowd are long gone. Dalymount Park has been slowly falling apart for decades now – without ever having been what you might call plush – and it is set to be replaced by a new compact stadium in the coming years. But having once attended an international game there in 1989 (for the friendly visit of France in a World

171

Cup warm-up game for Jack Charlton's Republic of Ireland), not long after its capacity had been more or less halved to 22,000 for safety reasons, I can well imagine just how loud and hairy the ground must have been for fans and players alike when the attendance surpassed the 30,000 mark. Indeed, on that night, as the crowd swayed, a little uncomfortably at times for my tastes, I did wonder just how on earth they squeezed another 20,000 souls in there for the biggest of games.

The grainy photos of the 1939 Cup Final in the various newspapers of the day record a sea of grey and grainy faces. But it's worth taking a little time to try and see past the black, white and grey of those images and to try and hear the roar of that mighty throng. See the team colours, the ruddy faces of the fans, the green sward, the red and blue flags, the matchday costumes of the supporters. Hear the prematch bands, the rattles, the chants, the songs, the cries. And feel the big-match tension in a heaving cacophony. For this was very much a cup final in the best traditions of the great game, and one from a very raw, and often unrefined, era of the game.

But Dixie Dean had seen such crowds before, and with regularity. And he had played in the biggest of games. And as *The Sligo Champion* recorded in the dressing rooms in the moments before kick-off, he appeared unfazed by a fixture that for many of his team-mates was the very biggest of their lives.

But given the circumstances – the stage of his career and the certainty before arriving in Ireland that such occasions would come no more – it wouldn't be too far wide of the mark to suggest that he would have experienced just a tingle or two of excitement to have found himself playing in a cup final once more in front of a very large and excited crowd.

Regardless of how he may have felt, Dean's renowned sense of calm allowed him to go and do what the great players do – attack the game, impose himself on it, influence it. This was the kind of event that he was born to, after all. And as the match reports suggest, Dixie gave his most impressive display in his time with Sligo Rovers in that first half. He was the focal point of the westerners' attack. His clever movement and slick and decisive distribution caused Shelbourne no end of trouble. And it was surely no surprise to anyone that it was he who put the Bit O' Red in front and apparently on the road to FAI Cup glory.

However, in the second half, it would be fair to say that he, along with his team-mates, faded as they struggled to maintain the intensity of their first-half onslaught (but as we'll see, the drop-off in Dean's performance levels was by no means inexplicable).

Nevertheless, a little less of Shelbourne's luck and a little more precision and Sligo Rovers would have been home and hosed by half-time. But failing to make the most of your chances is so often punished in football. And even if it was a goal part freakish good luck part goalkeeping catastrophe that was to deny Sligo and yield Shelbourne another opportunity, then Dean and his colleagues could scarcely have complained given the destination of the cup was eminently within their control for so much of the game. They knew Shelbourne's goal should never have mattered. The Bit O' Red should have been out of sight at that stage. The FAI officials should have been tying red ribbons on the trophy.

So both clubs would live to fight another day – Wednesday, 3 May to be exact, a week and a half away. And after all the furore and angst in Sligo over the original date of the final, the advantages, real or perceived, of that Sunday date were irrelevant now. The midweek fixture would make the trip to Dublin for Rovers fans a much more awkward affair, with Shelbourne supporters sure to fill the gaps they'd be leaving behind on the Dalymount terraces.

And there were two other worries for the westerners. Shelbourne would be able to welcome back the talismanic Tom Priestley, who had been unwittingly at the centre of all the controversy in the run-up to the original final. But surely more worrying for Sligo were the doubts that emerged in the aftermath of the drawn game over Dixie Dean's fitness for the replay.

15

No Time to Think – Dalymount and Dalymount Again!

THE SLIGO Rovers players barely had time to ponder their disappointment at letting such a wonderful opportunity slip through their fingers. Just three days later, they had another date in Phibsborough, this time in the last fixture of their league campaign – against Dalymount Park's custodians, Bohemians.

They did so knowing that the League of Ireland runners-up spot was on the line, and they were forced to face the Gypsies (as the Bohs are affectionately known) without Dean.

As it transpired, their cup-final hero had picked up an ankle injury during the match and had to be treated at the nearby Mater Hospital after the game. The knock may well go some way to explaining why Dixie had become less and less influential as that game wore on.

The injury was assessed again in Sligo Surgical Hospital on the same day that his team-mates faced off against Bohemians in Dublin. And an anxious wait would ensue over whether he could recover in time for the cup-final replay the following Wednesday – 3 May. But the Sligo Rovers committee were naturally determined to give him every chance and decided to leave a decision on his fitness to the 11th hour.

Without their star forward, Rovers battled hard to earn a point that saw them finish their league season ahead of Dundalk by a nose – albeit the Louthmen had a game left to play. Two goals down with half an hour left on the clock, the Bit O' Red stormed back to earn parity with a brace from William Johnston. Their fighting spirit on the day will have given their fans something of a lift – suggesting that even if Dixie failed to make the replay, their boys could still achieve FAI Cup glory. However, with Dundalk set to finish out their season with a trip to second-bottom Cork City the following Sunday, many felt that the runners-up spot was gone.

The Lilywhites were firm favourites to triumph over the struggling Cork side at the Mardyke and thereby leapfrog Sligo into second place behind champions Shamrock Rovers. But football so often has a surprise up its sleeve, and Dundalk failed to take advantage of their rivals' slip, managing only a draw themselves.

The result handed Sligo Rovers second spot – by the slimmest of slim margins. Both sides had finished on 27 points from their 22 games (nine adrift of the Hoops) but Peachey, Dean and their colleagues nicked the runners-up position on goal difference – and in the process achieved the second-best league finish in the club's short history.

News of Dundalk's ultimate stutter was naturally very gratefully received at the Showgrounds – quite the boost with the cup-final replay only three days away.

And maybe, just maybe, having smiled on Shelbourne in the first matchup, Lady Luck was now turning her gaze westward.

* * *

On the morning of the replay, the daily papers had little doubt that Sligo Rovers remained favourites to lift the cup. And another bumper crowd was expected at what was to be the first midweek replay of the FAI Cup Final.

The game was set for a 7pm kick-off. But despite the fact that many would be unable to travel from Sligo for the match, the growing interest in football and attendances in general suggested the stadium would see a healthy attendance all the same.

Indeed, the recent exploits of Ireland's representative sides (both the international[10] and League of Ireland 11s) and the crowds that had been in attendance (the League side's victory over their much-fancied Scottish opponents drew 35,000 to Dalymount) suggested that a paying audience close to that of the drawn final was expected.

Having been passed fit to start in the Sligo Rovers side, the presence of Dixie Dean was once more sure to be a big draw for the neutrals and the plain curious.

For WPM of the *Irish Independent*, it was the return of Shelbourne's Tom Priestley that dominated his preview

---

10   The Irish international 11 had beaten Poland and Switzerland and drawn with Hungary over the course of the season to that point.

of the game. Interestingly, the paper's soccer writer suggested that the winger's availability would be a relief to both sides. The Ringsend club's supporters would be naturally buoyed by his return, with many sure that had he been available for the first game, a replay would not have been necessary. And for Sligo Rovers fans, there had been a sense that should they have won that game, some of the shine would have been taken off the cup given Priestley's unavailability.

That said, WPM was of the opinion that the return of the international winger would likely make little difference to the eventual result. Sligo Rovers were, in his view, the superior side, had shown that clearly in the first encounter and would surely show it again in the replay. Do their jobs and play their game, and the Rovers players would be bringing the cup home to the banks of the Garavogue River and the heart of Sligo town.

'It was only downright bad luck, in my opinion, that kept the Westerners from piling up a commanding lead in the first half. They proved themselves the better football team on the occasion, though all honour must be awarded to the Shelbourne defence, but my belief is they will never miss such scoring opportunities again.

'Sligo Rovers played grand football in the drawn game. They cannot repeat their faults in regard to shooting in this game, and it only remains for them to give a repeat performance to lift the Cup.

'The form team is Sligo Rovers. The lucky team is Shelbourne, and there will not be much between the sides when Mr Hartles blows his final whistle tonight.'

And so the stage was set for another enthralling encounter. All Sligo Rovers had to do on their third visit to Phibsborough in ten days was play their football, take some of the chances their stylish attacking approach would surely yield and glory would follow. That was the theory anyways!

* * *

As things transpired, it was Shelbourne who were to start the brighter on that May night, grabbing an early goal before many of those in attendance had managed to settle themselves into their Dalymount surrounds. Their flying start saw them earn a corner in the first minute – the danger averted by alert goalkeeping from Sligo's Cranston – before planting the ball in the back of the Rovers net only seconds later.

A handball from O'Connor gave Shels a free kick 22 yards out, directly in front of the Sligo goal. The westerners hastily formed a defensive wall, while Shelbourne's full-back Sacky Glen stood over the ball and surveyed the scene. Noting that Cranston appeared to be a little unsighted and unsettled by his defenders, the veteran shaped as if to strike the ball to the keeper's right, before thrashing the ball inside the left upright, beating Sligo's stunned custodian all ends up. The Ringsend side were not at all cowed by their opponents' favourites tag. Game well and truly on.

Jolted into action, the westerners responded well and were almost on level terms minutes later. Glen's attempted clearance rebounded off the pressing Monaghan only for

Shels keeper Webster to produce the first of many fine saves on the night, pushing the ball round the post for a Sligo corner. The Bit O' Red began to turn up the heat and came desperately close to an equaliser soon after when Dean's goalbound drive was blocked by the brave Shelbourne captain Bill Little. And so the tone was set for the evening, as Sligo dominated the exchanges in their search for parity.

Time and again, however, Webster thwarted them in that first half, his most notable intervention a terrific double save, first denying Began, who had been released by Dean, before bravely scrambling away O'Connor's follow-up. The goalscorer, Glen, also played a key role, clearing the ball off the line twice as Shels battled against the Sligo tide.

Naturally, much of the focus before the replay had been on the return of Tom Priestley for Shelbourne. But for all the hype and expectation, the Belfast winger failed to fire his side on the day in an attacking sense. Having started brightly, he was starved of the ball as the Connacht side got on top before fading against the physicality of Sligo's defence, becoming little more than a peripheral figure as his side mounted a concerted rearguard action.

The chances kept coming as the Bit O' Red held an iron grip on proceedings, with left winger Monaghan guilty of passing up two presentable chances just before half-time – both created by the inestimable Dixie Dean. But if Shelbourne's players believed they had weathered the storm in reaching their dressing room with their lead still intact, they were in for a rude awakening, as

Rovers cranked up the tempo and the intensity to even higher levels in the second period in their search for the equaliser. It seemed only a matter of time before they would overturn the deficit and overrun their opponents.

The second half, delayed as fans spilled on to the pitch from a packed terrace, saw a continual bombardment of the Shelbourne goal, as Volt reported 'hair-breadth escapes' as plenty of 'shots were blocked, smothered, pushed away and punched out'. Began skimmed the crossbar with a drive, before the Bit O' Red fans thought their men had equalised on the hour. Dean, with his ankle heavily strapped and showing signs of discomfort, found the galloping Monaghan down the left wing. Sligo's wide man looked up before centring for Johnston to sweep the ball home. Cue relieved celebrations from the western contingent around the ground – only for their joy to be cruelly expunged by a shrill blast on Mr Hartles' whistle. The goal was ruled, somewhat controversially, offside.

Volt wasn't sure, but admitted he wasn't best placed to judge. However, post-game, the Rovers' forwards assured him that Johnston had been definitely 'on'. NAT, in the *Evening Herald*, agreed.

But Sligo were unbowed, and on they came in waves. In fact, Cranston in their goal was almost entirely unused in that second half – fielding the ball just once, from a Peachey back pass, relegated to the role of anxious bystander. The game was being played almost entirely in Shelbourne territory, with the westerners leaving only defender Daniel Lievesley to patrol their own half.

And still the chances came. Dean sent in a bullet header from a Began corner, only for Glen to stick out a foot and deny what looked a certain goal. The excitement grew, the din from the packed terraces deafening. 'Continuously came a roar for Sligo which is maintained to the last,' recalled Volt. 'The team plays even harder and Shelbourne wilt under the terrific gruelling.'

But the hardy men from the Ringsend club refuse to yield. And then right at the death, Dean is there, and a goal looks certain, but the brilliant Webster is there too and thwarts him once more. And that's the last chance for Sligo. Shelbourne earn a free kick. The pitch is invaded as the Dublin side's fans believe the game is over. A delay as order is restored. The free kick is taken. Little punts it long upfield, and that's that; there's time for no more as Mr Hartles blows the final whistle.

Shelbourne are in ecstasy as the Sligo Rovers players slump to the ground. Their incessant pressure has come to nothing. Their hopes dashed. There is no fairy-tale ending to the season for Dixie Dean and Sligo Rovers. The fairy tale will be Shelbourne's to tell, as the Ringsend side win the FAI Cup for the first time in their history.

'Scrambling on to the pitch,' recounted Volt, 'the Dublin fans cheer and cheer, rising Glen and Little to their shoulders, the green of Dalymount disappears under a black rushing mass of humanity. There are terrific cheers as the Cup is presented to Little, cheers that last for minutes and soon after Shels supporters dislocate traffic in O'Connell St as they proudly march the Cup to Ringsend.'

Looking on enviously at the Shelbourne celebrations, how Dean and the Sligo players must have regretted letting slip their lead so late on ten days before. How they must have cursed their own profligacy. And how they must have damned the clear bias of Lady Luck, who had surely taken up residence down in Ringsend that spring. For somehow Shelbourne had emerged victorious from a Sligo Rovers pummelling to win what many believed was the best and most enthralling FAI Cup Final to date.

'The better team does not always win,' wrote the disappointed Volt in *The Sligo Champion* the following Saturday, 'a saying that was proved to the hilt at Dalymount Park on Wednesday evening ... That Shelbourne are the luckiest team ever to have their name inscribed on the Cup is a fact their most ardent supporter would be prepared to admit.

'Favourites all the way, they fought with a tenacity that staggered Shelbourne, made the second half an agony of excitement for the crowd of 30,000,[11] and then lost gallantly to a team they outclassed in practically every department.

'A snap goal, enough to shake the spirit of a steel-nerved team, gave Shelbourne the lead. Holding on to that score for the remaining 88 minutes, Shelbourne accomplished a defensive feat that was at times brilliant, at times lucky, but at all times thrilling.'

---

11 The actual recorded attendance was 28,369 – a record for a midweek club game in Ireland at the time.

Socaro in the *Irish Press* told a similar story. 'A goal in the second minute of the Cup final replay at Dalymount Park gave Shelbourne the F.A. of Ireland Cup for the first time in their history, but no team has had to withstand such heavy pressure in order to realise their ambition.

'That Sligo Rovers should have won handsomely– from the territorial point of view–is no exaggeration.'

Sligo's inability to capitalise on the many chances they created was their undoing. It almost cost them in the original final, and they paid dearly for it in the replay. NAT summed the game up nicely in his report in the next day's *Evening Herald*: 'There was a succession of thrills as the ball flew by the posts or was scrambled away from the goalmouth and a few times literally out of the net during Sligo's frantic efforts to avert defeat. Their failure, however, cannot be attributed to luck. Their inability to score was, even allowing for the marvellous defence of their rivals, due to lack of shooting power and a finish to round off their clever football.

'The Westerners, in the circumstances, must regret not making full use of their opportunities in the drawn game, which they should have won in a walk.'

NAT, however, didn't include Dixie Dean in his criticism of the Rovers' forwards but picked up on a theme that arose right back in late January when the striker made his debut for the club – the inability of Dixie's team-mates to read his intentions and see what he saw at vital moments. 'Sligo proved once more that shooting is their bad suit. This weakness became even more acute through impetuosity when desperate in the closing stages. Dean alone remained calm, though he took – and gave – some hard knocks in bouts with Glen. The England international went near with some clever headers, his chief value was in passes to inside forwards, who failed to anticipate his intentions.'

However, it would have been fair to say that Dean was unable to influence the game in the way he would have liked. He was clearly lacking the mobility remarked upon by all the reporters from the first final. And as things transpired it was hardly surprising, for his heavily bandaged ankle was protecting a small broken bone in the joint that he had injured in the first meeting of the sides ten days earlier.

But in truth, unfortunate as that was, he and his team-mates knew very well that they had created enough opportunities in the replay to have won two matches. And they knew also that they should never have gifted Shelbourne a second opportunity.

16

The 'Dean Dividend'

WITH THE season finished, few suspected that Dixie's late chance in the replay would be his last meaningful intervention for Sligo Rovers and the last ball he would kick in anger in Ireland.

Indeed, well into the summer of 1939, with the war clouds gathering over Europe, Dean was still on Sligo's 'list of retained players', according to the *Irish Press*'s Socaro. The 'retained list' referred to those players who were out of contract with a club but whose registration was still retained by said club as they viewed the individual as being potentially worth a transfer fee if moved on. Socaro also noted in his paper on 6 July that Dean himself had also told him in a telephone call that he would welcome the opportunity to return to Ireland either as a manager or player-manager if the opportunity were to arise.

So it would appear that Dixie still harboured hopes of a return to action in Irish football, even if it might not be with Sligo Rovers. Moreover, at that stage, Sligo Rovers felt that if he were not to return to the Showgrounds they might be able to claim a decent sum of money from any Irish club who made a play for his services.

And in classic transfer tittle-tattle fashion (the game really hasn't changed all that much), the *Irish Press* reported that the Bit O' Red were already making contingency plans, busily looking at bringing in another big-name striker to replace the former Everton man, should Dean not be heading back to Connacht.

Incredibly, the paper named the club's main transfer target as none other than Arsenal's talismanic goal-getter and England international Ted Drake – and even went so far as to suggest that a deal had already been struck! Clearly, the transfer silly season is not just a recent manifestation.

'Who'll be Dixie Dean's successor as leader of Sligo Rovers' attack this coming season?' asked the paper. 'Our information is that it will be Ted Drake, famous Arsenal and England centre-forward. Peachey, the Rovers' centre-half and captain, who was commissioned by the club to go across the Channel in search of players is hot on the track of the Arsenal leader and hopes to get his signature. Our information, which, however, we cannot confirm, is that Drake has actually signed for Sligo, but this should be accepted with reserve for the time being.

'Ted Drake is probably the most spectacular centre-forward in the game to-day. He has been the Arsenal's top scorer in their great triumphs of recent seasons and has the hardest drive in English football.'

The *Belfast Newsletter* had also picked up on the story. And while they noted that the signing hadn't been confirmed as of 10 July, they didn't seem to bat an eyelid at the thought, going so far as to suggest that such was the revenue accrued from Dean's successful stint at the club that Sligo might well be in a position to pull off the deal! They even wondered why Northern Ireland's Irish League sides weren't looking to follow suit and engage in similar transfer strategies.

Drake, 27 at the time, had been Arsenal's top scorer in each of the previous five seasons and had won two league titles and an FA Cup in that period. The Sligo committee's brilliant coup in bringing Dean out of retirement and into the west had been a huge shock on both sides of the Irish Sea. But further success in enticing the Gunners striker, at the height of his powers, into the Irish game would have been a jaw-dropper of even more incredible proportions.

That said, the gulf in spending power between Irish and British clubs at the time wasn't anywhere near as pronounced as it was to later grow in the succeeding decades. In fact, as Irish clubs were not hampered by the maximum wage rules of British football and nor were they bound to respect the 'retained lists' of clubs in England, Scotland and Wales, quite a few good-quality players were enticed to cross the water into Ireland in the 1930s and 1940s. Some Irish clubs were able to offer very attractive – if not always sustainable in the long term – deals for those interested in making the switch. Moreover, as the British 'retained list' players could be signed on free transfers by Irish clubs, many did just that.

Granted, the trade worked both ways, as British clubs and those in Northern Ireland were also not restricted by the 'retained lists' of their League of Ireland counterparts – they too often lured good and very good players away for nothing. Indeed, according to Irish football historian and writer Gerry Farrell, there were many cases where clubs in Northern Ireland signed players from the League of Ireland for nothing with an eye to selling them on to English or Scottish sides for a sizable profit.

So, in a way, the idea of Sligo Rovers looking for quality players across the water was by no means outlandish. However, enticing a top player at the height of his powers away from one of England's biggest clubs would have been an eye-opener for sure.

Ultimately, however, the deal never materialised. And given the rather jaundiced eye with which we view transfer talk in the modern era, it's hard not to wonder whether the whole story might have been created to sell newspapers. There was truth in the idea that the Sligo club's committee were considering whether a move for another headline signing would be sensible or even feasible, but the idea that they could bring in a player of the calibre of Drake from one of England's best endowed clubs, the 'Bank of England club' no less, was surely fantasy. And so it proved.

Days later, surely one of the most bizarre transfer links in Irish football history was put firmly to bed. According to the *Irish Examiner*, Mr George Allison, manager-secretary of the Londoners, didn't mince his words in telling the paper's special correspondent that the Drake link was 'really stupid'. *The Sligo Champion* had also been on the case, shedding a little more light on the story. Alf Peachey had indeed been dispatched to England to scout players for the new season. However, according to the paper, the chairman of the Sligo Rovers committee had told them that the club's player-coach had not 'mentioned anything about Drake' in any of his reports back to the Showgrounds. Furthermore, the committee chairman couldn't confirm the report to the local paper that 'Drake's services were being sought', adding that none of the committee could do so either.

The *Champion* threw in a quote from the puzzled Mr Allison for good measure: 'The report is all Irish to me.'

* * *

Where the sources for the Drake story came from, indeed if there really were any solid sources, is unknown, but as mentioned earlier, Sligo Rovers were considering whether they could or should try and repeat the 'Dixie trick' for the 1939/40 season. Moreover, as the *Belfast Newsletter* had suggested, the club had done particularly well in financial terms out of Dean's four months in Ireland, as the club's annual general meeting in June confirmed.

The meeting, attended and recorded by a reporter from *The Sligo Champion*, offers an excellent insight into the running of a provincial League of Ireland club in that era and more importantly, for our purposes, into the impact Dean's presence had on the club's income that season.

Most striking perhaps was the input of the club's honorary secretary and treasurer, Andy Dolan, who noted that at the previous year's meeting 'there were questions over the ability of the club to run a team in the League of Ireland' at all. As ever, wages and the other usual running costs – monies paid out for rent, the upkeep of the facilities and pitch, the heating of the dressing rooms in the winter, travel costs – continued to place a serious burden on the club. It was pointed out that travel alone to the team's various 'engagements' amounted to over 6,400 miles for the season just finished!

In fact, as Dolan explained, the club had gone into the 1938/39 season with a debt of £423 (around €30,300 today). The monies owed weighed heavily on the minds of the committee members. However, when the parlous state of the club's books became known, a number of the club's 'friends' stepped in and 'gave handsome donations' to the tune of £140 (circa €10,000), allowing the club's committee to commit to giving the local, loyal fans another season of League of Ireland football. Dolan suggested that the club's supporters 'would remain ever grateful to those gentlemen for their generosity'.

For posterity and for their crucial role in later underwriting Dixie Dean's signature in the winter of 1938/39, I think it's worth listing those Dolan named and thanked on the night: Mr W.A.G. Middleton (£25); A. McHugh (£10); T.P. Toher (£10); J.G. Madill (£10); W.J. Smyth (£10 10 shillings); Major C.K. O'Hara (£5); Dr

Leyland, Boyle (£5); J. O' Doherty (£5); T.J. McGoldrick (£5). And we should also salute those 'others from the town and county', whose names' Dolan was not at liberty to disclose, who donated the other £55. Without these gentlemen, Sligo Rovers would not have had a League of Ireland presence, let alone a professional team in 1938. And they would not have signed one of the greatest strikers ever to have graced the game. And I'd have had no book to write on the incredible events of that time!

The club's benefactors were also thanked by chairman district justice Charles Flattery at the annual meeting, who pointedly added: 'When it came to taking the plunge and engaging the services of "Dixie" Dean, the same body of men were prepared to shoulder the responsibility for his wages should the venture not prove a success. Any committee which failed to make a success of their job with backing of that description deserved to be called an incompetent body of men.'

Considering the gambles made by the club and the successes of a season that saw Sligo Rovers finish runners-up in both of the Irish game's top competitions, *The Sligo Champion* reporter recorded the chairman as saying that 'the balance sheet spoke for itself'.

'On the expenditure side, the members would note that wages and bonuses had increased considerably over the figure paid in the previous season. The risks taken by the Management Committee in paying those increased wages were, he [the chairman] thought, justified by the results.

'However, Chairman Flattery was of the opinion that it would be financially impossible to run a team in Sligo without incurring an inevitable loss of £400 or £500 [€28,500 or €35,000] in a season unless the team found itself figuring in the final of the Cup. He had learned that gradually, and from his experience, he had every reason to believe it was true. It was futile to talk about enlarging stands, altering the amount of members' subscriptions or any of those things, because the economies that would result would be infinitesimal compared to the outlay of fielding a team good enough to attract the public.'

The Sligo Rovers chairman, however, believed that the burden on the incoming committee would be even heavier than it had been in the past, because in his judgement, it was becoming increasingly difficult to make football attractive – particularly in the provincial outposts of the Irish game.

Having grown up in the era when it was said that interest in football on this island, or rather in its weekly attendance, had been eroded by the advent of televised football from across the Irish Sea, it was interesting to read what threats a League of Ireland chairman was concerned about in the apparently buoyant game of the 1930s.

In this case, it wasn't the growing interest in Gaelic games or indeed the attractions of any other sport that concerned district justice Flattery. Rather, it was the stars of the silver screen and the comfort of the cinema houses that were popping up all over the country that were threatening to undermine support for the people's game and impact the numbers passing through the gates.

From the *Champion*'s report, 'In many provincial towns where senior football was played, it was found that in the cinemas there was a strong counter attraction to the appeal of football. Men who had worked hard out of doors during a week could not be blamed if they preferred the comfort of a cinema, with its heated and comfortable atmosphere, to the rigours of the Showgrounds on a wet cold day.'

But despite the looming threat from Hollywood and the big studio houses in Elstree and Pinewood across the water, Sligo Rovers had succeeded in ending the season with a credit balance. 'They had run certain risks,' said the chairman, 'and an element of luck had brought about their success. But the Management Committee had paid off every known debt, and so far as they were aware, they owed nothing.' In fact, having gone into the season with that worrying debt of £423 (around €30,300) on their books, Sligo Rovers' finances experienced a mighty turnaround to finish with a healthy credit balance of £516 (€36,900).

William Ralph Dean's signing played a major part in what had been a bumper season for the club – and it's also clear from the gate receipts recouped from their FAI Cup run and the three Dalymount Park appearances that Mr Flattery's views on the importance of the domestic knockout tournament were well founded.

The Bit O' Red's treasurer Andy Dolan's financial report on the night showed that the club earned the following net gate receipts from Irish football's three main competitions that term – the Shield, the league and the FAI Cup:

Shield games: £593 6 shillings 11 pence (€42,600)
League games: £1,040 4 shillings 9 pence (€74,600)
FAI Cup games: £1,505 9 shillings 8 pence (€108,000)

There are a few things worth noting here with regards to the 'Dean dividend'. The striker arrived in Sligo in late January after the club had already played its 11 Shield fixtures and met ten of its League of Ireland appointments. The club did see a boost to its coffers in the remaining 12 league fixtures, particularly those in which Dixie figured – but it was the monies generated by the westerners' involvement in the FAI Cup that ultimately cleared Sligo's debts and pushed them comfortably into the black. And it was with a view to having such a cup run in the second half of the season that Sligo's management committee gambled on signing the Englishman in the first place.

But what really stands out from the club's revenues from the three competitions is that Sligo Rovers earned almost as much from their five FAI Cup games with Cork City, Distillery, Dundalk and Shelbourne as they did from the 33 Shield and league games they played that season!

Dean's presence on the pitch played no small part in the Bit O' Red's drive to Dalymount Park, and it was a crucial factor in bringing combined crowds of over 80,000 to Phibsborough for their semi-final and final appearances and the relative riches accrued by the westerners as a result. No wonder they generously sent him home on the boat to Liverpool with an envelope reported to contain £80 sterling (€5,500) to keep him company. He had most certainly deserved his piece of the pie. And remember, in English top-flight football at the time, that represented around ten weeks' wages for a top player. Dixie certainly didn't forget the Sligo committee's generosity, telling the *Liverpool Echo*'s Michael Charters some 30 years later that it 'was a terrific amount from a little club like Sligo and I was very grateful'.

For the coming season, however, the Bit O' Red's hierarchy had to decide on whether they should commit to a similar model as in the season past – or whether they would need to retrench somewhat. Could they afford to gamble on another signing like Dean and count on negotiating a similarly lucrative cup run?

District justice Flattery believed that it was possible – but admitted that there were external factors in the year ahead that foresaw a changed local landscape.

The club was a popular and well-supported institution in the town and surrounding areas – but he felt that it was important that all involved recognised that Sligo Rovers could not take priority over a community and town that was trying to develop, grow and modernise. Sligo, after all, was desperately in need of new schools to accommodate its growing population, and much of the money to build them would have to be raised locally.

Flattery pointed out that as a result the club would be less able to raise money for the running of the organisation from the usual community fundraisers – the sweeps, raffles, dinner dances and, crucially, the fundraising carnival that was held at the Showgrounds each summer. The importance of the carnival to the club was borne out in the accounts, which showed that Sligo Rovers had benefited to the tune of £109 (€7,800) from staging that event alone the previous summer.

For the chairman, the club's needs would have to be secondary to those of the town and its people. Any carnival on the Showgrounds would have to be run to help raise funds for the building of schools. As district justice Flattery put it to those assembled at the club's AGM, Sligo Rovers 'would not be acting fairly if they contemplated a counter-attraction'. And that went for the other fundraisers too – all of which would have to be run sparingly in the season ahead.

'The new committee would have to decide whether they would follow the policy adopted during the previous season or develop a policy of cautiousness and conservatism which would mean economy in wages and in every other possible way,' reported *The Sligo Champion*'s man at the gathering. However, the paper noted that Flattery thought it would be 'worthwhile to have a discussion broadly on that issue'. His own informed opinion was that it would be worth the risk 'and if the same risk were taken in the coming season in fielding the best possible team, he did not see why the committee would not have the same measure of success'. As it happens, and it's a story perhaps for Sligo Rovers historians to write about, the club's committee did push on in the following season and with some success. The Bit O' Red performed well in the bread and butter of the 1939/40 league season, garnering one more point than they managed the previous term, although they did drop a position to finish third.

But in the FAI Cup, they did repeat the trick of the Dean season, reaching another final – only to suffer yet more heartbreak, beaten soundly by three goals to nil by Shamrock Rovers in the decider. To soften the blow, however, the club coffers profited not only from their cup run, but also from taking a cut in what was then a record crowd for the Irish game's blue-ribbon tie, as Dalymount Park bulged with an attendance of some 38,500 football fans.

17

The Curtain Comes Down

DIXIE DEAN returned home to Nottingham and his family in May 1939 unsure of where his future lay. But as the summer progressed, it was clear that he still harboured hopes of staying in the game – and as we saw, he was open to a return to Ireland if that was where the best offers would come from. That said, with a wife and young family to look after and re-engage with, staying in England was preferable. His Sligo sojourn had suited well in terms of timing – not only had Dean recovered from the injuries that had put paid to his time at Notts County, but the offer to play in Ireland meant he'd only be away for three or four months. Were he to return for another season, well, that would either require a longer period away from home or result in greater upheaval and a move of lock, stock, barrel and family across the water. Neither was ideal.

But the strange and wonderful final years of Dean's professional football career were set for another surprise twist, before being definitively ended by Adolf Hitler's catastrophic European adventures and the outbreak of World War II.

Bizarrely, little Hurst FC – a non-league outfit in the Cheshire County League – signed Dixie in August and in doing so made him one of the best-paid players in the English game at the time!

Such were the subversive effects of the maximum wage era in English football. Although professional players in the Football League (Division One, Division Two, and Division Three North and South) had their earnings capped, those operating outside of those four divisions were not bound by such restrictions. And so by dint of not being members of the Football League, Hurst were able to offer Dixie a lucrative last hurrah.

Dean made his debut at the Greater Manchester club's Hurst Cross ground on 26 August 1939. And as with Sligo Rovers, his presence swelled the attendance, allowing Hurst to reap record gate receipts from a crowd of 5,600 spectators, softening the blow of their 4-0 defeat. By all accounts, Dean's decline was now more than apparent – the lack of a proper preseason and the crumbling and aching joints taking their final toll on his playing career. But his eye for a goal and his finishing prowess were still in evidence a few days later when he bagged a textbook header in a 4-1 win for his new club.

And then the affairs of the world intervened. Having already annexed Austria in March 1938 and the Sudetenland in Czechoslovakia in the autumn of the same year, Hitler directed his armies to invade Poland on 1 September 1939, just a few days after Dean's first appearances in Cheshire. The subsequent refusal by the Nazi leader to respond to Neville Chamberlain's ultimatum that they withdraw led to a British declaration of war on 3 September. World War II had begun. Soon after, professional football in England ceased and with it the playing career of William Ralph Dixie Dean at the age of just 32.

* * *

With the Hurst deal suspended and Britain now at war, Dean and his family decided to move back to Merseyside to be near their relatives and friends. Perhaps a return to neutral Ireland, where football was still being played, might have crossed Dixie's mind. However, with his country in need, any such move would have been an affront to the ideals of any patriotic man. So to support his family while he awaited the inevitable call-up to aid the country's war effort, Dean had to look for work. This was the harsh reality faced by the vast majority of retired professional footballers of the time, even those of legendary status. Indeed, many players – even those lucky enough to have a multi-year contract with a club – often worked in the summer months to supplement their incomes. But for those who had hung up their boots, there was no safety net, no living on their career earnings, and little or no support from the club or anyone involved in their former profession.

With opportunities scarce, the humble position the greatest goalscorer English football had ever witnessed was to attain and occupy for the next few months showed just how difficult life could be for those who knew little or nothing from a young age other than the beautiful game.

Only four months after walking out in front of a crowd of almost 30,000 in his last game for Sligo Rovers at the FAI Cup Final replay in Dalymount Park, Dixie Dean debuted in what Nick Walsh described as a 'menial and dirty job' in the lairage of an abattoir in his beloved Birkenhead.

'It might have been thought,' wrote Walsh, 'that this local sporting hero would have no difficulty in obtaining an easier and more lucrative kind of employment, but stars of his profession meet the inevitable fate of becoming forgotten in economic terms when they lose what they once had to offer.'

Dean was to remain in his job in the abattoir until he was called up for army duty in 1940. During the war years, many famous sports stars who saw service did so as physical training instructors, with rank and status, and rarely if ever saw any action. According to Walsh, 'Dean did not seek such advantages and went into the infantry as a private, joining the Kings (Liverpool) Regiment and doing his primary training at Formby near Liverpool.'

He later volunteered for a transfer to the Royal Tank Regiment – utilising knowledge from his formative years working with his father as an apprentice fitter on the Wirral Railways – to become a mechanic instructor with the rank of corporal on tanks and Bren gun carriers. He was initially based in the rather aptly named Warminster in Wiltshire, before transferring to the 27th Lancers in Yorkshire. Dean recalled in *Dixie Uncut* that his unit travelled all over Britain but focused on home defence, so he never saw combat.

The one oddity of Dean's war years was how, despite his legendary status, he was never invited to play in any of the many representative football games that were organised to entertain the troops and the public and that featured many of the British game's stars. It's hard to credit, but perhaps those in charge were of the Red persuasion? Who knows? But his omission from such events was somewhat strange.

Dixie did play some football during that period, however, turning out occasionally for his own unit. He did recall one other match in which he featured as a guest player for Cambridge Town against an RAF side. Cambridge won easily – 15-1. No prizes for guessing who bagged eight of their goals.

When the war ended in 1945 and Dixie was demobbed, his next move was straight out of the football cliché handbook for retired footballers of the 1960s, 70s and 80s – he took over the running of a pub.

'During the war, my home in New Ferry had been blitzed and my wife and three children were living with a couple in Chester,' Dean recalled in *Dixie Uncut*. 'My wife decided we had to get out of that, get in some business and start to make our own lives again. Now I had to find myself a new job. There was nothing left for me in football.'

Dean had an old friend in the brewery business who helped set him up in a public house called the Dublin Packet in Chester's main square close to the Town Hall. Boots well and truly hung up, Dixie and family stayed there for 15 happy years. Indeed, the pub became something of an attraction given the star status of its landlord. According to Nick Walsh, 'stars of sport, stage and screen frequently called in to pay their respects'.

Same old Dixie Dean – always pulling a crowd.

* * *

It was early into his career as a pub landlord that Dean was to get a pleasant and welcome reminder of his time across the water in Ireland. One morning, almost seven years after his last game with Sligo Rovers in the FAI Cup Final replay with Shelbourne, Dixie received a small parcel in the post with an Irish postmark. Out of the package, to his great surprise, rolled his runners-up medal from that day. It had gone missing at the reception for the team after their unfortunate defeat all those years ago.

'A crowded hotel function room which he attended demanded the showing of the prized runners-up medals won by the Sligo team,' Walsh tells us. 'The medals were duly passed around a cheerful, exuberant and intoxicated group of supporters. By the end of the evening, Dean's cup medal had not been returned and the conclusion was that it had been purloined. Dean, who had always been diffident about such symbols and honours won at sport, reacted to the situation without fuss. But the club, officials and many supporters became very much concerned, and as their pride in Irish hospitality was injured, they made every effort to recover the medal but without success.'

No note or explanation of any kind came with the returned medal. Was it taken by some unthinking supporter with a bit of drink taken, absent-mindedly put in a coat pocket and forgotten about in all the excitement and hubbub – only to be discovered many years later in a spring clean? Or was it possibly returned to its rightful owner due to a guilty conscience finally getting the better of someone who should have known better? Given how it arrived at the Dublin Packet, that somehow seems the most likely suggestion. Whatever the real story, one can only imagine the smile on Dean's face once he realised what the package contained and the memories flooded back of those happy few months playing for the Bit O' Red and living the life of a footballer in the shadow of Benbulben with all its imposing beauty.

In 1961, Dean gave up the Dublin Packet and returned to Merseyside. On getting wind of his return and his need for employment, John Moores, the football pools tycoon and chairman of Everton, stepped in to offer Dixie a job as a security guard in his organisation's buildings in Liverpool. And there, the Everton legend, the club's record goalscorer and the greatest marksman ever to grace the English game, humbly worked out his time, rising at 4.30am every morning to be in work for 6am, until his retirement 11 years later in 1972.

Moores is also credited with helping organise a long overdue testimonial for Dean in 1964 – some 25 years after the player had left Goodison Park under something of a cloud. Many Evertonians had been left uncomfortable at the fact that the club's greatest-ever player had exited without the traditional thanks that great servants were due. Indeed, up until recent decades, the testimonial was crucial to the immediate futures of any players facing retirement given their limited career earnings and future prospects. Dixie's sudden departure and his fractured relationship with club secretary Theo Kelly back in 1938 meant he had been denied that honour. Moores was determined to right that wrong and celebrate publicly Dean's part in Blues history in better-late-than-never fashion.

Goodison Park was the venue for what was to be a unique occasion on 7 April 1964 – as 'Liverton England' (a team made up of English players from Liverpool and Everton) played 'Liverton Scotland' (a selection of Scots from both clubs) in front of 40,000 fans. The game reportedly raised a sum of £7,000 (€146,000) for Dean and his family, much of which was used to buy a house – soberingly the first, according to his granddaughter, Melanie Prentice, that Dixie had ever owned.

Six years later, in 1970, while he worked in the Littlewoods garage-supply stores near Liverpool city centre, the esteem and indeed the affection with which he was still held in Connacht once again revealed itself. Sligo Rovers had reached another FAI Cup Final – still looking to bury their cup hoodoo 31 years after he had led them to their first appearance in the competition's decider. With Rovers set to play Dublin side Bohemians at Dalymount Park in late April, Dean received a rather generous offer from the brother of one of the club's honorary secretaries from the pre-war years.

Willie Mulligan had been synonymous with the club in those days and had done much to raise its profile. He had passed away the previous year. His brother, Martin, had been successful in the licensed trade in London and was one of many Sligo people being drawn back to Dublin for the cup final, hoping at last to see history made. And in conjunction with the club, he arranged for Dixie to be their guest of honour at the Phibsborough ground on the big day.

As *The Sligo Champion* rightly reported, 'It was a splendid thought for Martin Mulligan to bring this great player back to meet many of those who remember him as the most colourful and famous player to wear the red and white of Sligo Rovers.'

Dean was delighted to accept the offer, but as Nick Walsh recounted, the great man was not overly fond of flying. Ironic for a man who built his reputation as one of football's greats on his mastery in the air! But with all expenses paid and the airplane tickets bought, Dixie agreed to fly to Dublin for the weekend. And to help calm his nerves and in recognition of the exalted status of a man he saw as his most important passenger, the captain of the flight allowed Dean to sit in the cockpit and even take the controls!

For the record, the 1970 FAI Cup Final ended 0-0, although by all accounts it was at least a game full of incident for Dean to enjoy. Sadly for the westerners, however, their dreams of cup glory were once again to be dashed, with Bohemians taking the cup after a second replay.

In fact, those dreams were not to be realised until some 13 years later, when the Bit O' Red finally took the FAI Cup home to Connacht in 1983. Exacting revenge over the Gypsies in a 2-1 win, Sligo's achievement came three years after Dixie's untimely demise.

Dean, after several years of failing health, had somewhat poetically passed away while attending the Merseyside derby at his beloved Goodison Park on 1 March 1980. No doubt he'd have been watching and enjoying Sligo's good fortune from on high, however, when finally the cup was lifted bedecked in the red and white ribbons of the little club in the shadow of Benbulben that captured his heart so many years before.

18

Ties that Bind

JUST AFTER lunch on Sunday, 2 April 1939, Bill Cosgrave closes his front door and heads out to meet his brothers for the walk from Rathgar, a suburb on Dublin's southside, to Milltown, home of League of Ireland champions Shamrock Rovers. Bill and his brothers have trodden this path, made their little pilgrimage, many, many times. It's their ritual whenever the Hoops play in Glenmalure Park. The meeting, the chat and the 25-minute walk down through Dartry, under the Nine Arches Bridge and up to the ground.

But Sunday, 2 April 1939 is set to be a special one. Rovers are on the cusp of retaining their League of Ireland title, and becoming the first club to do so. A draw will probably do it, and confidence is high. But the game will be doubly special for these football-mad men – because the visitors are Sligo Rovers, and amongst their number is the greatest goalscorer the game has ever seen – William Ralph Dixie Dean. Bill Cosgrave was my mother's dad, my grandfather, and a man I never met. Bill died at the tragically young age of 47, a victim of the scourge of tuberculosis, eight years after Dixie graced the Milltown sward. He was a passionate football man who never missed a Rovers home match, and as a little girl, my mother remembered the Sunday afternoon routine well. She, like her two siblings, also caught that bug and they would often accompany their dad to matches when they were old enough. Exciting and fun Sunday afternoons with Bill, days magnified in meaning later with his untimely death.

All three would continue the regular trips to see Shamrock Rovers and others as they entered adulthood. Indeed, my late and dearly loved Uncle Jim, Mam's elder brother, actually graced Glenmalure Park and Dalymount as a reserve-team player for both Shamrock Rovers and Bohemians in the 1950s. In fact, as I wrote this book, two photos of Jim positioned on the shelves above the desk in my office proved inspirational. Robbed cruelly of his memories by age and dementia in his latter years, the pictures magnificently and evocatively capture him playing for Bohemians in his prime. The images were taken at Tolka Park. In one, my uncle is beating the last defender and has the keeper and the goal in his sights. In the other, he's outfoxing the man between the sticks with a looping header. How he loved to recount tales of such derring-do!

The fabled Drumcondra ground was almost empty. It was reserve-team football after all. Regardless, both photographs are impossibly romantic and magical for me. Making that grade should be seen as the serious achievement it is. I even played in a few games at that level myself as a student – albeit as an impostor in the Trinity College Dublin ranks, reaping the benefit of staying at home to work in the college's library in the summer of 1992. The coaching staff had little option but to give me a run with the League of Ireland B season kicking off a month before the college term and the return of their preferred starters who had spread out across Europe and America for work and summer fun! Nevertheless, the substitute appearances against University College Dublin, St James's Gate, Monaghan United and St Patrick's Athletic were the pinnacle of my football 'career'.

If people scoff at the quality of League of Ireland footballers – and they do – then they'd have little time for what were hugely memorable moments for me, and they'd have precious little time for the achievements of my dear old uncle. But anyone who shared a pitch with men who had played in the league, even in the 'stiffs', will know just how good these lads were. Dismissing them as players who were not good enough to go across the water has never been fair.

My late father was also a Shamrock Rovers fan. He would cycle to every home game he could from working-class Crumlin. He did so long before he ever met my mother. When they were courting, the two would often make a date out of a match. And although he couldn't kick snow off a rope nor hit a cow's arse with a banjo, as Mam often put it with a fondly knowing smile, he was accepted into her family with ease because of their shared passion for the Hoops and for football.

In the early years of marriage, they would still go to see games. But life stages dictate so much of what we do, and having six kids of their own reduced the opportunities and the energy to make the trips in the 1970s and 80s.

By the time I arrived on the scene, number five of six in 1971, their League of Ireland days were all but done. But as I grew and became more and more obsessed by football, mainly of the English variety I'll confess, I did manage to coax and cajole them into taking me to a few games. My three brothers were also heavily invested in football, but none of them had any interest in going to the domestic offering, unless it was a preseason friendly involving Liverpool, Manchester United or Nottingham Forest.

However, I was a little different. Any football would do. And that included the domestic fare – even if for some or almost all of my peers, such desires were clearly those fuelled by some form of madness. But while outings to games were often very irregular, largely limited to FAI Cup finals through the dog years of the 1980s, they are still cherished memories for me.

The love I have for football is a gift bequeathed by the grandfather I never met through the daughter he never saw grow to adulthood. Although my dad and his family were also football fans, it was the infectious way in which Mam loved – and in her mid-80s still loves – the game that arguably influenced me most. And that came directly from her father.

She often still tells me of how he and her uncles would return home after games and talk and talk at the kitchen table of what they saw. Of how they would use coins, knives and forks, cups, saucers and whatever else came to hand to replay the major incidents. She even recalls how she was instructed in the intricacies of the offside rule with the salt and pepper pots deployed as educational aids, as her own mother, who had little time for such trifles, rolled her eyes in bewildered dismay.

That grounding in the game, in the chat and in the fun, manifested itself in the natural joy and good humour she's always exhibited when football is on the menu. And it was passed on to me in turn – well, maybe not always with the same sense of joy or phlegmatic acceptance! (Although I have mellowed over the years, I promise.)

Before I started to research the story of Dixie Dean's time in Sligo, I had no idea that my own grandad had been there in Milltown to see him play. That fact was only uncovered as I chatted to Mam about the tale, her face lighting up at the mention of Sligo's visit to Glenmalure in April 1939 as she realised that this must have been the time her father had seen one of his great heroes play. After all, he had told them about it often enough!

That realisation – the very notion that my grandad was there – proved something of an inspiration in the times when I toiled in researching and writing the story of Dixie's Sligo sojourn. As kids, my nana – Bill's wife, Rita – was a major presence in our lives. But grandad Bill was so long dead, so long gone, that it was almost as if he didn't exist. I guess when someone is gone over

20 years before you were born, that's natural. He'd be mentioned from time to time. He smiled out at us from a small picture on the mantelpiece in Nana's house and does so still, seated on his deckchair, on my mother's fireplace. But he was a mystery. Not forgotten by us, just not known.

But the very idea that he saw Dixie Dean play in Milltown that spring day has created a slender link across time between the two of us. And the more I've thought about him standing on the terraces that day, the more my grandad Bill has come into view. And when Mam told me that he would have so loved to be remembered in this way, the reasons for writing and continuing to write the book became clearer, sharper in my mind's eye.

Because football is about so much more than matters on the pitch. Football is family, it's your parents, it's your siblings, it's your grandparents, it's your children. It's your friends. It's the stories, the laughs, the talk, the empty seats when those with whom you enjoyed the game are gone. It's the comfort, the structure, the routine. It's my grandfather Bill. It's the delightful Melanie Prentice's grandad Dixie Dean.

But football is also folklore. And Irish football, with its long and colourful history, is as steeped in folklore as any other. The story of the great English centre-forward's four months at Sligo Rovers is but one example.

William Ralph Dixie Dean almost certainly came to Ireland for the money. And although he was full value for it (11 goals in 11 games and his numerous assists certainly underlined his worth on the pitch, and the rude health of the club accounts after his departure showed his value off of it), his stay came to mean so much more to him and to those who witnessed it.

Those four months in the winter, spring and early summer of 1939 may just have been a short chapter in his storied and legendary football career and in the long history of the Bit O' Red, but they had an enduring resonance for both.

Dixie Dean – Goalscorer

-   60 league goals in 39 English Division One appearances (1927/28)
-   67 goals in 46 league, FA Cup and international matches that season
-   100 English Football League goals before he was 21 years old
-   200 English Football League goals in 199 games by the age of 23
-   349 league goals for Everton in 399 games
-   377 league and FA Cup goals for the Toffees in 432 matches
-   37 career hat-tricks
-   Over 20 league goals in nine consecutive seasons
-   More than 30 league goals in four seasons
-   27 Division Three North league goals for Tranmere Rovers in 27 league games as a 17-year-old (1924/25)
-   11 goals in 11 League of Ireland and FAI Cup appearances for Sligo Rovers

Dean is third on the all-time list for goals scored in the English top flight, with 310. Only Jimmy Greaves (357 with Tottenham Hotspur, Chelsea and West Ham) and Steve Bloomer (314 for Derby County and Middlesbrough) rank ahead of him. However, Dean's goals came in just 362 matches for the Blues, whereas the Greaves and Bloomer totals came from 516 and 535 games, respectively.

Dean's tally of 310 top-flight goals is still the most by a player for a single club.

Dixie played for Everton over 14 seasons. All but one of those were in Division One. In the 1930/31 term, Dean and Everton were in Division Two. Dixie scored 39 times in 37 league games that season, with another nine in the FA Cup.

Sligo Rovers Results
1938/39 Season

Date	Comp.	Opponents		Score	Goalscorers
21 Aug	City Cup	Bray Unknowns		1 - 3	Began
28 Aug	Shield	**SHELBOURNE**	H	5 - 2	Began 2, O'Connor, McGivern, Graham
4 Sep	Shield	Limerick	A	2 - 0	Began, Dykes
11 Sep	Shield	**DUNDALK**	H	1 - 1	Began
18 Sep	Shield	Drumcondra	A	3 - 2	Began, White, og
25 Sep	Shield	**CORK**	H	1 - 1	White
2 Oct	Shield	**WATERFORD**	H	1 - 1	Mitchell
9 Oct	Shield	St James's Gate	A	2 - 5	Johnston, og
16 Oct	Shield	Shamrock Rovers	A	1 - 2	White
23 Oct	Shield	**BRIDEVILLE**	H	3 - 1	White, Graham, Began
30 Oct	Shield	**BRAY UNKNOWNS**	H	2 - 2	White, Began

6 Nov	Shield	Bohemians	A	1 - 1	McCready
13 Nov	League	Shelbourne	A	2 - 3	McGivern, White
20 Nov	League	**LIMERICK**	H	3 - 0	Began 2, Johnston
27 Nov	League	Dundalk	A	1 - 1	Johnston
4 Dec	League	**DRUMCONDRA**	H	1 - 0	Began
11 Dec	League	Cork	A	2 - 0	Monaghan, O'Connor
18 Dec	League	Waterford	A	1 - 1	O'Connor
26 Dec	League	**ST JAMES'S GATE**	H	5 - 1	O'Connor 2, Began 2, Monaghan
1 Jan	League	**SHAMROCK ROVERS**	H	0 - 1	
8 Jan	League	Brideville	A	1 - 1	Monaghan
22 Jan	League	**BOHEMIANS**	H	4 - 0	Monaghan, Johnston, White, O'Connor
29 Jan	League	**SHELBOURNE**	H	3 - 2	Monaghan, **Dean**, Clarke
1 Feb	League	Bray Unknowns	A	1 - 2	**Dean**
5 Feb	League	Limerick	A	0 - 3	
12 Feb	FAI Cup	Cork	A	2 - 1	Monaghan, Hay
19 Feb	League	**DUNDALK**	H	1 - 1	O'Connor
26 Feb	League	Drumcondra	A	1 - 1	O'Connor
5 Mar	FAI Cup	**DISTILLERY**	H	2 - 1	Johnston, McDaid

12 Mar	League	**CORK**	H	4 - 3	Thompson 2, Seddon, McPeake
19 Mar	League	**WATERFORD**	H	7 - 1	**Dean 5**, Seddon, Began
26 Mar	FAI Cup SF	**DUNDALK**	N	2 - 1	Began, O'Connor
1 Apr	League	St James's Gate	A	0 - 3	
2 Apr	League	Shamrock Rovers *	A	3 - 3	O'Connor, Johnston, McPeake
9 Apr	League	**BRIDEVILLE**	H	6 - 1	Hay 3, Johnston, **Dean**, Seddon
16 Apr	League	**BRAY UNKNOWNS**	H	2 - 1	**Dean 2**
23 Apr	FAI Cup Final	**SHELBOURNE**	H	1 - 1	**Dean**
26 Apr	League	Bohemians	A	2 - 2	Johnston 2
3 May	FAI Cup Final Replay	Shelbourne	H	0 - 1	

Acknowledgements

I'VE RECEIVED so much help and advice in this endeavour that it would be entirely remiss of me not to offer heartfelt thanks to all of those who played a part in seeing the project come to fruition.

Up front, I'd like to thank Melanie Prentice, 'Dixie' Dean's kind granddaughter. She gave me lots of encouragement and a lovely foreword for the book, all while working so successfully at keeping her grandad's legacy alive at The Dixie Dean Hotel in his beloved Liverpool.

The input from the members of the brilliant Sligo Rovers Heritage Group – Keith O'Dwyer, Kevin Colreavy, Joe Molloy and Aidan Mannion, in particular – has been crucial in putting the book together. Many thanks, gentlemen, for sourcing the wonderful photographs and artefacts relating to Dean's time at your great club. Special mention must go to Keith, who with such good nature marshalled the troops and answered my plaintiff pleas for assistance across the months, and to Daragh Stewart, who located and sent on those magical images.

As the book is largely an historical account, I must also thank Gerard Farrell, Daniel Sexton and Gary Spain for their interest and invaluable insight into the early decades of the Irish game.

Finally, a brief word of thanks to Paul Howard, Jonathan O'Brien and Gareth Power for their sage authorly counsel and to Patrick O'Donoghue and Liam Hayes for pointing me in the right direction.

Bibliography

NEWSPAPERS AND ONLINE SOURCES
Irish Newspaper Archives
The British Newspaper Archive
The Sligo Champion
Irish Press
Evening Herald
Cork Examiner
Belfast Telegraph
Belfast Newsletter
Birmingham Mail
Derry Journal
Evening Echo
Liverpool Echo
Liverpool Evening Express
The Times
The Guardian
Irish Independent
Sunday Independent
These Football Times

ToffeeWeb
Irish Golf Desk

BOOKS AND REFERENCES

Walsh, N., *Dixie Dean – The Life Story of a Goalscoring Legend,* Macdonald and Jane's, 1977

Dean, W.R. and Charters, M., *Dixie Uncut – The Lost Interview,* Trinity Mirror Sport Media, Kindle Edition, March 2013

Busby, M. and Hutchins, D., *Soccer at the Top: My Life in Football,* Weidenfeld and Nicolson, January 1973

Mannion, A., Molloy, J. and Kilfeather, A., *The Bit O' Red – A History of Sligo Rovers 1928-2016*, Sligo Rovers Heritage Group, 2016

Also available at all good book stores

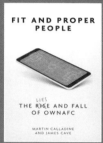

FIT AND PROPER PEOPLE

LIES

THE RISE AND FALL OF OWNAFC

MARTIN CALLADINE AND JAMES CAVE

9781801500470

AARON MOORE

FIELDS OF DREAMS AND BROKEN FENCES

DELVING INTO THE MYSTERY WORLD OF NON-LEAGUE FOOTBALL

9781801501002

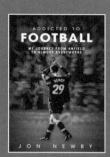

ADDICTED TO FOOTBALL

MY JOURNEY FROM ANFIELD TO ALMOST EVERYWHERE

JON NEWBY

9781801500739

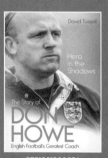

David Tossell

Hero in the Shadows

The Story of DON HOWE

English Football's Greatest Coach

9781801500876

WE MADE THEM ANGRY

Scotland at the World Cup

Spain 82

TOM BROGAN

9781801500906

JONNY BRICK

From Kids to CHAMPIONS

The History of the FA Youth Cup

9781801500913

EMANUELE GIULIANELLI

QARABAG

THE TEAM WITHOUT A CITY
and Their Quest to Conquer Europe

9781801500920

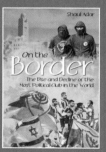

Shaul Adar

On the Border

The Rise and Decline of the Most Political Club in the World

9781801500951

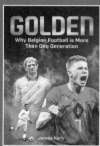

GOLDEN

Why Belgian Football is More Than One Generation

James Kelly

9781801501057